AMERICAN
FLOWERS

TYLER FLYNN DORHOLT

DOCK STREET PRESS

SEATTLE

www.dockstreetpress.com

Copyright © 2016 Tyler Flynn Dorholt

Dock Street Press and colophon are registered
trademarks of Dock Street Press

ISBN:978-0-9910657-9-0

Printed in the U.S.A.

for Katie Jane

in memory of Michael Trossman & Wendy Weil

The fragility of the flower
unbruised
penetrates spaces

—William Carlos Williams

                              Mysterious
perfections, like flowers, but all, all as we can
know, give, take down address of, felt in the (bred
in the) bones.

—Alice Notley

CONTENTS

But if it is possible to make pictures of the "core" as well as the struck-off sparks of the subject, this is a picture-story. —Henri Cartier-Bresson

ONE (11-49)

As it begins ... I take it there ... I hang out for you ... Above the ground ... It continues ... At the back ... To wait it out ... That he's dead already ... A memento ...You have to grip the presence ... Think now ... In the street ... To leave it tied ... At the wall ...You see another side ... You were not supposed to ... Between trees ...Sorted as to soon be ... We are at a beach ... The automatics ... Your belongings ... It's time to arrive ... Outside of the open ... When we came to ... Curiosity is the arc ... Without the show ...That your lovers line ... Please come brawl ... The same hold ... Light making it in like this ... I will crawl out ... Hold your breath ... Suddenly the rain up on you ... Full recline ... We can't get through this ... War is the beginning ... Nests unraveling ...Whether or not you're ready ...We came through this war ... I hold you because ... Loaded in the real ... I want to tell you where I am ... In the crowd, restless ... Such is delicacy ... His eagerness a reward ... She makes a new field ... In larger color ... Longer ago than ... When push comes to move ...

TWO (51-91)

Carrying another star ... Low shorts, shade ... We had it in mind ... Marching ahead of the myth ...You cannot get it right ... She ran her palm against ... As you have held the world ... Pull your dream ... At the back the take ...Who knows what it's doing ... A live show ... The other world that shuts ... Move over here ... It's another day ... Letting you in ... Because the other light ... The wheel halved ... Put on your warrior ... In another light ... Now, as you see yourself ... Come into the shade ... They slid down ... That the other life might ... Hang us around here ... Land on your back ... We allow it ... Fuck you full moon ... When the body opens ... I asked her ... The center splinters ... I've been meaning to tell you ... Nobody knows if they'll be ... In here, as you reflect ... The first step, throwing ... The small hand-picked ... They will give you the vessel ... And the other option ...You wing a holy light ... Operating the way it does ... Please relieve me ... As it continues ... The old world, sea-spotted ...

THREE (93-135)

As it gets to be as it never was … Come along to knock … The body that you hold … Months later … To cut a hole in the world … Build it to be on it … Tower in, flower out … From the sea … As they will come to … They all see me leaning … Be even quieter … Again, this neighboring … He calls it solace … What you cannot stand … Start them lined up … Everyone untying their … Come back, sweet thing … Along the lines of all … They take you out … I've been there … That the mountain being there … That you can & will take the head off … Down along the mall … In the middle of it again … I have not told you yet … Border of the other … She wants nothing to do with it … In the crowd you cannot hear … It is still there on the corner … Serious about the brawl … Shape as we undo it … When the horses are gone … The rein returns … Both here, one with the shirt … And another America … You can't splay it that way … Last age in the look …

FOUR (137-177)

The glass window trusts … This, the other task … Above, how the roads are … Lining up for the appreciation … Responsibility, as it takes … Handling the pipes … As if to retreat, poked … Slip or the arch hanging … For centuries, just … Time for another … It's the same year but … The pride is readymade … Consider again youth … Yes me, no you … Over in the song quiet … As the first thing you do is silent … It's the only glowing … Slip in, get the days … When the shadow remains … And here in the interlude … They will tell you a painter … Cleared out … Oh & for everything to lie … From reflection this is our mistake … Sure enough, I've been in a river … Found it there curled … Your envy of the tree … A long smooth leg … We stuff the flowers … Dear Light … She sits down to draw … Can't figure it, can't … At this high lean singing … She's thinking & the world … I confess now … And patrons overseeing … As all background … I return to you … As you know, as … The crack in the room … You hold the bird in your hand … All stacks into face … The interlude is exuding the cloth …

FIVE (179-215)

What you feel as the breeze ... Following the heat ... Between the last
... Your eggs & toast ... Let us slow down again ... On the frequency
... But you must understand ... Moving with what you want ... Before
he is taken ... Tracing from a cup your hand ... He will keep the heart
in ... Think first as a destructible ... Protect us here ... We said goodbye
... It hasn't changed ... Grace be hands ... You know what the lover ...
Dear Light, I return ... Questioning it by leaning into it ... Suggesting it
by pulling back ... Along the line of all ... Coming along to where life
lowers ... Lean in right around here ... War is always in the middle ... As
we are driven ... From this plot, up again ... We meet in the back room
... I can't veer where you are ... If it will be ready ... He plays it casual ...
What I have to play ... You come out of your homes ... Forget if they're
listening ... As we wonder about ... As wild as it can be ... To see it
going down & care ... Go harder now ...

SIX (217-255)

They've arrived to capture ... This is where you dodge ... On the
rocking chair ... Harder now to follow ... At the front, standing ... And
then the back ... She doesn't want to go ... This far into the narrative
... Lining up to leave ... All those who have passed ... When we begin
... Flight, how at once ... Consider the farm ... But still here ... The
news is coming out ... They haven't begun ... That this looks good ...
Sit inside a vessel ... At the gallery the two lovers ... Careful not to call
it into ... Reflection is no different ... It's the morning after ... As giant
as you can be ... All day the balloons rising ... It's not difference but ...
These are the cross streets ... Sure enough, I'm here ... If we pause here
it still goes ... Consider the dome around ... Respecting the disease we
become ... Are we more ... That you will meet me ... Why can't you
remain ... Getting it together ... You turn the culture ... Guitar mood,
ranch breath ... As it ends it begins again inside ...

ONE

LORENCE IS A ...
FIGHT AT SIGHT ...
WE SLIP OUTSIDE OF WHAT ...
THE MOST FORGETS ABOUT
MOST IMPORTANT MAYBE ABOUT
THE TOMATOES, WE'VE ARRIVE
HANDS IN THE ...
TIPPED ON OUR TOES

THINK NOW ABOUT ...
SCULPTURES, WHAT STONE
LEAVING RIVERBEDS TO ...
RESIDENCY, CORPORED AND
MADE TO THE TOWN ...
SUP OF YOUR LIFE ON ...
BICYCLING ALL THIS WITH TO
TO WATCH YOUR TIRES ...
DISCONT, AS GOOD AS ...
CLIMBING UNDERWATER ...

SORTED AS TO SOON BE ANOTHER
OTHER, NUMBERED BY RATING AND
THE APPARITION OF REPPERE, ...
IS THE FIRST STOP OUT OF THE BLUR,
UNZIPPING THE CODE AND RUBBING A
NECK OUT OF ITS NIGHTLY CATCH, TO
... IN SIMPLER MEETINGS TO BRING

WE CAME THROUGH THIS WAR ONCE
BEFORE, OF NOT UNDERSTANDING WHO WE
ARE ANYMORE, YELLING FOR INFORMATION
ABOUT OUR PAST AND WHAT REASON

3.05.13

PLEASE COME BRAWL OUT YOUR
WINDOW, THE SONG FROM ONE TO AN-
OTHER ALWAYS TRANSLATION MAKING
ITSELF AN INSTIGATION, A S TO RUBBLE
THROUGH SQUARES AND AROUND YOURSELF
A DOOR THERE, TO OTHER POCKETS OF
LYNCHING THE WORLD, TINTED RECLUSION
AND RETIRING INTO EACH NIGHT WITHOUT
... DESIRE TO COME OUT OF IT READY TO
UNDERSTAND THAT IT IS NOW, EACH THING YOU
DO, AND YOUR LONG LEGS THE LAST THING
THE LIVING SEE, BRICK RETURNING TO
DAMSEL SCRAPS, HOW FAR YOU MUST BE

SUDDENLY THE RAIN ON YOU, SLAIN
DOWN REMAINS UPON YOU, THERE SLIPPING
LIGAMENTS SWEATING THROUGH
FILAMENTS, RED MADE OUT ...
SOAKED IN GELLED CLOAK OF
TEAR ALL THE CLOTH AWAY ...
VALLEY OF THE HIP CUT THROUGH
THE TIP OF THE NAIL, THE ...
BUTTON PALM INTO THE TH...
WE KEEP COUNTING THE RAIN ...
FOR OUR EYES CUTTING THE TR...
STARE OF LUST, A LINE OF RAIN YOU CAN
RUBS THE SICKLY SLIP OF BRICK INTO THE
BED OF A CLOUD AND CLI...

LONGER AGO THAN WE ...
FORWARD WITH, SHORTER IN
WIDTH THAN WE CAN TIP OUR
FOR THE CODE, ALL THE STARS
BOWL OF RICE OR A ROLLING
LEG DOWN YOUR SPEECH ALLEY,
EVEN MORE FROM THE SHARP
THEY PUNCH THROUGH WALLS TO

SIDE BUT I WILL CRAWL OUT
WINDOW, THE LINES I'VE DRAWN
THE CURVES OF MY FACE YES
..., LONG-NAILED AND DIRTY, TO
... THE RURAL VERNACULAR
... GUESTS TROUBLE THESE PARTS
..., THIS INVITES INTO THIS ... COMES BACK AS
... CHOKE BECAUSE
... LONG ENOUGH ..., HAVING BEEN LAUGHING IN SYNC
DISREGARDING ... SOMEONE IN THE BACK OF THE
... THE STARS ... AT THE MICROPHONE REFERENCE
... THE BORDER, ...THE SPEAKERS SELECTING SOLO

IN THE CROWD, RESTLESS, TO
LEAVE NOW WITH ATTICS, TO
MOVE ON WITHOUT THE SENSES
AS THE TREES BEHIND THE
HOUSE KEEP BRUSHING WINDOWS
AT NIGHT, MAKING MOVEMENT
OVER AS IT TOO CAN BE
ABANDONED AT THE WRONG
TIME, STRIKE THE CAMP MAKES
LATE UNTIL SOMETHING UNDER-
WATER URGES IT ON TO SHORE,
WE WHO STOKE OUR BISHOP
IN OUR GUEST IN OUR PILLOW
COMES SWELLING FROM THE
OUTING, WHERE IN OUR
ROAD THE CLICK WE CANNOT
DROWN STICKS THE TEETH INTO
GRASS, RIGHT BEFORE WE MOVE.

As it begins it begins again within us, shadow the light sweeps flat, to pretend that when the eyes open we don't carry on here as lovers, gloved in the last slope the water moons away from, originality fumbled into dust, to swoosh a silent scuttle upon the rooftop dusk, while in the squares & ovals below us the world closes into its shelves, voices un-spun in the labor-gush, the audience fondling scarred coins, pushing the faces back into cheekbones, the felt-lipped line of our legs slitting the sun into relapse, as we come again to dance behind ourselves in the middle of the unsayable, while outside of our bodies, over the gate & in the fields, rain drives the sides of our lives spit by spit, into the holes in which with worlds we sit, senseless but unshaken by the hands that hold our leave.

I take it there sometimes, to again, over into an us, or how again is a hanging shape, what drums through us as all the others try to undo us, even as we stand stilled & undone as one, eyelids slipping quickly in fatigue, to continue in sight through the lips where silence bowls out, gatekeeper of the language that tastes good alone in the throat, portaging the breath to where the tongue thrums, stone of the shallow speak.

I hang out for you here, in my hero hair, my zero chair, where I've swung ideas & resemblance from other affairs—trust in alleyways, what dries out in contention with layer, wanting only that flap in the spin, that sparkle in the root of periphery where truth peaks—into the mend, pretending into song, clawing nude at the texture of the sun's slant in the back pitch & run, waiting for the ghosts to unwind from inside the clothesline.

Above the ground, in this game, the fame that is left to mitt the glimmer with, or if from here all things dim into slimmer solos, the chorus for the invisible contour where we are ignored in the afternoon tour of history—that noxious float of good wood—as all that's after this threatens to lessen us—the wind that stays in a dress to keep a graze on the thigh, symposium, what before this came right after us—but we can still spill back from the lean & remain, sun on a smoke-break by the jukebox.

It continues, reach & what for—waving rain back up the walls, to sink the roof from the top & pop off the blinks—grain in the field untouched by wind, as passing around us are the thinner hands the city licks into buttons, crushing from function, letting light say yes & no & maybe & never again, as the glow of our arrival pertains to localities just outside of survival, our clothes folding loosely over bones but not home, cleft where we ought to start out on our own again, replete with drowned air.

At the back of your stance a rupture, the gap in a line I climb out of mistakes from, turning other hurried waters into hush, holding the heartier rope toward your rise in my hands—a thought grope, a mind hope—smacked back by minutes to chance the paddle of the ponder, muscles w/o objects, putting the boards up for the ceremony of time to keep inside itself, in the clipped grid with personal thud, our eyes against the glass until it smashes & the sea flakes in, our arms around the shore, unfound but rising for more.

To wait it out, to cover up & go under, to fashion through angels, sleeping in any position just to sleep, to creep past the self, the ballad that stops for the boyishly trumpeting pause, spending the entire day grooving the thought back into a circle for when the lights don't return, as returning is never the turn, as we don't feel images upon the face as a place we're coming back to—freckle in time, idea inside the seeing—giving a big damn about where the breath ends & if it is careening from where it began, or back, diving deep in the pivot of our sirens, returning to where our bodies box up before they rock out from their squares.

That he's dead already, the one you've looked up to, or for, running his mouth off at the ocean, untying his boots at the bar & the buoy, the garden you take care of just by watching, in nightfall what light between sight keeps telling us we become untraceable, fog romp, the bees fucking the flowers one by one until all that's left is a flag & yellow there, a thick flash of worry gashing the dance, to come beyond your eyes opening & slap the air out of its shape, its delirium, where the circles restore & we evolve in the revolving & natural gizmo, lotus & bud, spine & cobbled talk.

A memento is a lozenge, a lozenge a crescendo, & if we fight sight hard enough we swipe outside of what we comprehend, the most forgotten about but also most important thing about touching the tomatoes that they can fade, washing our hands off in the river & where that goes, tipped on our toes to drive stance through rows of red we'll need if we're to thrust ahead of pulse & greed, the sun & rain enhanced by the convulsions between, this worry & that failure, as we look like that rock if we stay put long enough in the stops, our palms the small walls only the openness between them can relieve.

You have to grip the presence backwards to come along in order, always room for street-side procreation, bricks lining up to forget about the earth between them, delicate as we are in presenting the negativity in optimism, that we don't think for others but are always doing, succumbing, opting to & for them, a paycheck behind patience & procrastination, the incessant strategizing in sudden borders, curiosity—that thinking into what looks known in the moment—inching against will & ability, thrill & stability, breathing as we can *en masse, en route* to the faith that isn't concerned with belief, the dog you walk around you when you're reeling for the cool down.

Think now about passing the cornerstone sculptures, what stone does leaving riverbeds—pretend residency—coppered & mistaken near mares in the town square, the stringy slip of your life on a shaky roof, the mini boom of being removed, bicycling to the waterfall to watch your tires perspire in descent, as good as they'll ever be grinding under water dams, past youth in celebratory memory glands, to pool out in lily & demand the passing canoes stoop to not cut through you, silk & swagger, how we destem every time we look at the sky, thinking we can lift it up & remain alive.

In the street I pause & I've done this before, relieved myself in the central flux, left myself at myself, content if deposited in what comes around sense, the statues less alone than what they celebrate, untouched for decades, shadow of a boat or a genital taking waves over for the fall, the wall waiting for the window to be changed so that it shows us the house that we're in, that the attic is no place for mourning, the kitchen not fit enough to withstand hunger, & that this is all that I can think of in the space of our release.

To leave it tied, to tie it on, to take history out of its misery on a ship & float there w/o purpose upon inhabitant, sideways like a tree trekking mid lake to wither, rain playing against itself on window panes, the air you abuse to halve that attitude & stuff that thought rudely within, finding out yesterday went by w/o sucking your pulp right, the last dirty retreat we defeat in this sculpt, to remain unchallenged by stillness, gifted to flummox in base needs, how you feel your waist quake in the song swish, & that it brings you under the waves that go over the waves that go over the waves that go over.

At the wall that keeps our shadow, at the carriage that stays put upon corners, in the staying that steers further in, upon the further from the farther out, colliding rocks & what the bored rural children do miles away from the farm on their bikes, tilling dreams, that we've been destroying things collectively in our sleep for years & the one window that completes this porch & form & culture—central as we're meant to be dealing with doors & floors—keeps opening & closing, inch by inch each day, reflecting us back at us, nothing on the other side outside of wind.

You see another side of yourself, the sea inside yourself, the blue outtake of being outflanked by blues, incised corridor for off-duty roaming, companionship transfer, sieving an eye or what comes to be in the others you hold in caring about the wand which is desire, swinging it in circles by yourself until the surface of another silence skids, pinning some core, some touch, that rattling hot button of a center or belief, the self, what you wish to push as the light goes hush.

You were not supposed to spiral, to call out identity as less heartening than the loss of it, as marked as we are to diminish in unfinished arcs, as is knowing this moment was not set up versus knowing it was, that the lie is that you don't live in between anything—a dimmer switch, a bicycle recycling stars as you round a gated-in block in all black, asking for clarity & sediment—but cement instead inside the walls, where the flash of fate rakes reason up into your lungs, stuffing it rung by wrung into the body bell that is hung.

Between trees, between avenues, against detail, against destruction, the hat that has it after you—coordinate of stadium smoke rubbed on ribs—pressed out of the teeth in chattering plume, how many ideas suffer between exhalations, against inhale, a heat wave coddling the undergarment, turning around in order to defend what has been left behind, the rewind of longing, that it started with image not making do with itself, wrapping a wooden frame around everyone you know during their sleep then hanging them on the tree, against the wall: when you release them can you decipher this movement at all?

Sorted as to soon be another, the additional other, away from yourself, numbed by lassitude, an apparition for the reduced mind, standing in the first step of passivity, out of the blur, unzipping the code & rubbing a neck out of its nightly catch, to fever in simpler meetings, to drive the solution into the middle of the street, stopping traffic with the giant hello, as going through the door is going through more time into less of yourself, what you did just then with your mind in the hallway defining time, sucking semblance up to speech, to the mouth in a word's last reach.

We are at a beach touring ourselves back to sand, shoulders no different than clouds & the walls, how they keep showing up w/o the other side, as we're looking hard enough to see through them but not enough to undo them, the bald halt between smoke rolls, another gate opening for the rhythm section of connection, this kind of city where silos ply themselves out of the untouched winds to halo before the overdose, to switch & to curl with storms out of the ditch of the norm, ringing a yell at that playable act, pitching a feel in that relatable fact, positioning grass to crank change back to certainty that cannot be passed, as all that we need out here is black & white, our skin brooked to ignite, our tension making senseless colors out of light.

The automatics are eating us away again—nobody can see the admonishing of the mannequins on Main Street, so past midnight my feet keep returning me to where I cannot reflect, a decision to stop all traffic & mime myself painting a wall, that none of these cars will move through what their operators aim to do, torsos always an extra chance at turning over the wonder of our cores, deeper in the street where I can roar up to your window demanding our whereabouts in the past & if there's a path from there to here, or to where I'm willing to go when I find my way back from reflect, to be resurrected & direct.

Your belongings around you & you'd flee w/o them for the nearness of lake & bird, away from sea & the herds that keep us continuing as being seen—transit, produce, appropriation, choice, monograph, denial, the flush throat of neglect—& within them the small prestige of liking the other, linking to but never coming through their clasp, raspy in the artifacts of heritage & impulse—still pears bruised by dusted lamps— but you're already a step over, where belongingness skates atop the roof, above the day, where planes keep dousing the vertical world away, & the fear is that you touch yourself out of it any which way.

It's time to arrive w/o the walls, to take the secret out of its mystery, the dream out of contingency, as we are meant to become more than just voice in echo, the unfinished song which is just thought having come along too late for tongue, that there's nothing to say when purity arrives, watching a glen or gorge cruise & gouge itself, & so you tell others that they should have been there with you when you weighed nothing at all, in desire & function, when even the water wouldn't reflect you because it was content with its shelves, ravished by sky & the future of movement, running down into a valley, miles away from the road, hoisting your head up in its hands.

Outside of the open, there's still a face in every window around this place, smiling in knowing that we're up to no good stringing bait on the look of our lines, passing always through something jumbo, clacking for skin tone or the hue of what our teeth feel when the tongue swipes out from touch—hair, the best defensive cover for the loss of ideas—that we are all on a glorifying venture alone & will die ready to repeat our lives but w/o time, choosing which window to crawl back into or out of, the threadbare beat of our feet opening the square in the wall for circles, booming beyond the mumble.

When we came to music we emptied the lakes & rivers & ran our nails deep into the walls, black & white paint stored in our shoes, scrounging for tempo, how streets crack back to remind the island of the buoyant bodyguard, the buttons on every shirt in the closet desperate to shake off string & gurgle the solo back to cantos, marbled & incendiary, rolling a pitch into compendium, this pendulum of vogue, the future running by with fingers patting the crops, drab flags in drafts of gleam, pulling a cloud down into perfect stare then collapsing in the water fountain, shining back up at what falls.

Curiosity is the arc, blown up for all the young ones to hang under, sweating in collars, flipped everywhere in the touchstone despair of youth, where you're unaware of why the world bursts out of itself, leaving you a cut-up house instead of a home, to throw more rocks at that which is clashing behind lock & schism, chasing them back to where they deflect & to then resurrect homage here, spinning the stick on the stone until the fires intone, protective of the disbelief that fills the pockets w/o the hands, marking up the past below the half-crescent, steeping the cure for what the land has obscured.

Without the show, the day in front of you as splat in the graph of depiction, that pleasure is nothing more than the mood you move through to remind yourself of where you subsist w/o it, wriggling into anxieties, tramping for the out-of-body, that bee stings will take you far away from where your head hangs—that safety bulge, see-socket—or how the shuddering & the fever are just the body grounded back into prayer, organized to make order there, as we pilot with a point & rise in a line even where direction is w/o time, this way for that thing, buttons & zippers, relief in the pop & clip, until we put on our shoes & drip out of it.

That your lovers line up behind one another in memory, cascading, or in from where you've been, squinting in the defying light, missing out on seeing what went down as the world gathered in the knob of a boxy feed, a leader of macro roams, sincere about oneself but with insecure exterior—sunglasses, bleached hair, crouched shoulders—or how easy it is to glide around judgment when there is no person or human-made objects cuffing your perimeter, the hammock release or the willow tree in its head-banging throw down against the ground, swift in the blackout, swirling around to the see & sway, lugging out lightly w/o your body in the day.

Please come brawl the skies from outside your window, the song from one to another always translation making itself instigation, as to rubble through squares & adorn yourself in doors you put the feeling in a jug & dip comments into other lockets for lynching the world, tinned reclusion & retiring into night w/o a desire to come out of it, unready to understand that it is new, each thing that you do, & your legs the last the living will see in the brash flee, bricks returning to damsel scraps of stone & ambiguity, how far you must be from yourself when every time the camera opens you grit down, expose, then bolt right back into your rows.

The same hold as desire only more delicate, wanting the time just as much now as then, when it missed you, the stripped lust of the spiritual, bunching clock ticks in lines & memory in pocketed pics, ears holed for the candled impresario, this decade's take on romance as the run of everything running out just before the fix, specifically cinema & geography, moving beyond limbs to their lens-less images, the music that pans out when you can't glow down, silk over pumping machinery, as forward as your personal foreigner can be, squeezed into glance, to discuss the peeled-away pall then run a palm across text & viscera, to grace the dance before the band gives up on chance.

Light making it in like this, last dusk's shotgun-echoing sun, the theatrical day bent on cauterizing civility, unease, a knife or a shoe horn for a tongue, hair growing through the nail to joint the shine, the vein of your resistance to insist on not being defined, cotton no different thirty years later than when picked, dying in flower patterns on your blouse, bracelet made out of tire rims in a decade w/o motor or mouth, that it's enough to let light slide across your back into those other eyes, that it is all you'll ever need to thrive, then die.

I will crawl out that window, yes, I will—I have yet to be outside of inside but I will crawl out that window, yes, the lines I've drawn into the curves of my face, the flowers that have flocked out of grace, yes, I will, long-nailed & dusty, complete the rural vernacular these guest houses trouble into conversational arts—this inside coral, this high-rise disguise, this beached choice—because staring at anything long enough leaves you at away.

Hold your breath & as you release it reveal what you've been dealing with inside your head, what hasn't felt real & is more than piecemeal pain, that your body unpeels its shake when you sleep & awakens to drape its take against societal mistakes, as squealing back in are the thoughts that have done you in, drowning always during the climax of the know, not ever knowing that face in the mirror, fearful of baths & traffic, to hold your breath & wait, close, plate it in thorough rows, or to share it with others before inside your mind it blows.

Suddenly the rain up on you, slain down remains upon you, these tumbling ligaments sweating through filaments, bed of felled oak, legs soaked in a gelled cloak of grope, to tear the cloth away & give in, out, valley of the hip cut through with the tip of a nail, the dive of a buttery palm into the triangles & squares, as we keep courting the rain, forgetting we are responsible for how our eyes cue pain, a line of water you can ride the sticky slip of, back into the bed of clouds & climax there, thundering in solo density.

Full recline, out of the cloth & into the skin, sensuous malleability below the riverbed, the restless dead, a flicker of flesh brushing atop the waters, reflection's mistress, floating lull, these circles that save worlds & voices then pace the rocks back to action, soft & in the whole plot crafted to rage off, the sun won over by what surface sends back, by the angle legs take teaching the water to ride around lack, to go under what was here, to wave, to experience w/o delay or crave.

We can't get through this w/o speaking of war, but which one I'll never know so the era ends & every silhouette gets sucked up by blown-down brick, your lover collapsed in it, heaving heavy air back through windows, that returning to anywhere is intruding upon your absence, trying to fit yourself into time as it is gone & so are the assemblages of breath you laid with foreign community, dirt making an excuse for earth by stamping the plaid shirt, your face a sergeant for the unshed jitters, wearing clicking heels to the funeral, taking them off & crawling right in with the casket.

War is the beginning or is it not the beginning of war to cover yourself in wind when the corner mouths enact streetlight—with impassioned voice ourselves above ourselves, then leveled back for choice, as we are diminished only by what goes unsaid or undone, not by what is happening, to partake in the eroding rope with its ends still intact, sprinting from younger speech in the barrel the bullet pulls exact, asking what the root rubs against, wherein begins the act.

Nests unraveling, minds leaping as bushels into behavior, to murmur into the roads where cars keep dying, knowing how to strip a tree down so that it becomes a warm lung in winter's crushing drawl, outside the zoo where it's hard not to call yourself an animal when you strike at the space between yourself & the mirror, terrified of how you got to be so near, this not knowing who that is there, taking wind out of time, that all the moments we don't have our eyes open in sleep means we don't see the light brewing & the circus spinning & the memory returning, or that it's just not us, ever or fully, only what we can discuss from in the flowering pulley.

Whether or not you're ready, you must now recall how a body will fall out of its shell in front of you—fog through bridge—& how life is too large a world to hold or hedge on strife's edge, even as the body passes out of its fold alerting you it can be clasped, to look at what you love knowing it won't lip past laugh or cast the query of glance back, this trackless expanse, as is feeling open in rain a way to lay the senses down plain, memory still in air for when you can't run your fingers through its hair.

We came through this war once before, of not understanding who we are anymore, yelling for information about our pasts & what religion ran like sand between our teeth, listening harder to the records than we have the passing pool of ourselves, our tone, our push toward companions & zones, dancing them into meaning & reference as the audience sits patiently, forgetting they are victims too—to be reprimanded for something inside your blood, then to skin out the letting, red as red as it ever will be, leaving your body entirely.

I hold you because the radio is broken & the damage is done, world rolling out of itself in numbers & catastrophes, the end of an era because it just started to sound right having our hearts chained in collateral brevity, the only man w/o a hat who keeps weeping & collapsing with microphone below the bell, recording his shakes, that we too shake in dread feeling the end of something overtake us, even as we were not in its beginning, as you are not in any absence made responsible for totality, the real that gets in the way when you get caught believing in a moment, smiling with grass in your hand.

Loaded in the real, as you've known darkness to flash out brighter than light, strangers marching into your spectacle to tell you peace has left the skies, that every circle will now square out & the fingers you led across a piano will stick up the unmovable trees, scuttling leaves back to bud, the hottest hour when you crank the lake backward looking for livable land, to rent out all feeling here, to be understood, for the slant in a long run around the short line, the grazing of something fine before the finish, before design.

I want to tell you where I am, staring into the fire we built to remember what has left us, parting from nothing more temporary than the field we cross in retrieving the extemporaneous, log on log for trees from forest, raising those hands up in the scream of bees, nobody ready for the inventors of peace or harmony to intervene with our unease, even if it's from their words where we can return to ourselves, flowing out stemless to picket the pointless sky, stock phrases in our never-tongues, the whole cinema slumping right when the hero steps on the bridge, & that we walk out there, between mountains, to the edges of the ridge, & take a picture of what cannot be seen.

In the crowd, restless, to leave now with ashes splashed upon our canvas, to move on w/o the source, as the trees behind the house keep brushing windows come dark then leaving, mulling night over, as it too can be abandoned at the wrong time, sticking the canoe mid lake until something under the water surges it back onto the shore, we who store our belief in our eyes in case relief comes searing from the inside, where in our bones the click we cannot disown sticks the truth right before we move, leaving us grooved in the away.

Such is delicacy to reminisce with utterance, hooking its tasteful lace on a statue's crook, the type of laugh you share with yourself & yourself only as the phonograph needle lifts & clicks, troubled ankle in the boot, finger on a stick, as we offer others more than what comes back as nostalgia, having been cackling in sync with someone in the back of the room as the hour references you, the selective solo for pills, bonked out from the throat in the looming heart, lent to repeat a beat from the mouth of a silhouette, bodiless in sweat.

His eagerness a reward to the self for consistently slinking up to duty, the body always more furniture than cloud, finding itself a noise deep in the dossier, flowers dead-set on arising in a balcony & the large appetite of a letter awaiting the poised vowels of pain, that we should suffer negatives while wandering about the wheels that carry soap & oil, a saxophone never quitting the wail as it leans in front of the distracted mirror to impale the sheen, still golden behind dust, hands cradling it beyond rust, busting out of straps.

She makes a new field all of its own & we line up to roam here, patterns running out of the particular into vehicular odes of vagary, clamping down on skin in a heel that crosses texture only to remember it must leave the body at night, selfless in any mirror as long as what surrounds us does not appear inside us—as the sentence opens up to be direction—that I am available in the night but not myself, our breath before becoming the bend in which lying down ends what we stand up for.

In larger color we leave a box for foreign arms, stripped down, a piano walking off the stage to glare again in the rear den, as if technology isn't just history's overgrown toenail, forced to jag & ditty as the spears plug blood dots between unspeakable reaching, pillars standing still all day before fisting midnight's jaw, or how we come out of train stations forgetting airs pop at leveled ground, pounding ourselves upward w/o a sound.

Longer ago than we can move forward with, shorter in the shallow width than we can tip over in looking for the code, all the strength in a bowl of rice or a rolling cube of ice down the speech device, others punch through walls to insist upon the sprawl of darkness, the dialogue & genre, as you can trace the arrival of any light given you're content feeling your way out of sight to where it's only temperature & shape, stars that earn themselves into the planet, sentenced to diminish in our lamps, to clamp onto our bodies & quiver.

When push comes to move we all have a story about protecting something invisible, as we must rethink ourselves, but just enough as not to drown the shelves into which we delve—maturity, that child, the moral hides of unfiltered sides, the pursuant & logical angel—& view is no more blessed than a splotch of seaweed vanishing in conch, no greater than a sealed book, but equal to what museums do to indefinable oils coaxed into frame, as spitting would be a photograph for you were the tongue in touch with the landing, as what I have done, just in seeing, to insult an endless roam, walking across seeing w/o looking, working for nothing but advance in knowing that it is shared, that even though the drink makes you speak past yourself, conked out on preparation & fantasy, & that what you remember next will be how great the time was where memory lasted & you upheld it w/o recasting it.

TWO

HG HAD IT IN HIS MIND HE'D REMIND WITH TIME TO FORGET THE LAND, BREAK DANCING WITH A FLAG, A DIFFERENT ACCENT + TARNISHED COLOR, FULL LICENSE TO SEPARATE IN DELICACIES WHILE THE SANITY OUT THROUGH, AS IS SUPPORTING THE'S THINGS ABOUT A STADIUM ELEVATIONS, PRACTICAL IN THE LOW LAND TO REMAIN A BIT WHILE THE VESSEL LINES DOWN THE KNOWN ROAD, WISHING A GUITAR WOULD COME MORE FULL INTO THIS...

SHE RAN HER PALM AGAINST THE ENTIRE SHORELINE AND SENT HERSELF BACK INTO THE MIDDLE, THE PLAYING FIELD THE PLANED FIELD THE PLAIN FIELDS, HOPES TO STRAIGHTEN INTO LAKES FROM MATTERS, NO RHYME CAN REMIND, A TREE SOMETHING TO STAND ALONE AND AROUND WHICH YOU CANNOT BE FOUND AT ALL, HER PART AT THE TOP OF THE HILL TO BE REFILLED,

THE HIGH
BE A CRICKET,
... OTHER
IN YOUR FEET
... OF THE
... TO LEARNING
... PATH
... AS
... IT
... ALREADY
... FOR
ANOTHER TO

CARRYING ANOTHER STAR PER CONSTELLATION MAKING THE DREAM WHERE YOU'RE HOME AND GOES IN, AS WE'VE BEEN LONG THIS WHO DOES NOT THING TO PROGRAM A SPURT OF GREEN GRASS ON SWIM, MAKING REVOLUTIONS LONGED TO ART THE CONCEPT WE WHO COME OUT OF DOWN FORWARD YEAR, TAKING TOO

AT THE BACK THE TAKE, THE OLD SKIN I'D LIMBER OF BREAKS FOR CHURNING OTHER FLURRIED PETALS INTO GUSH, FOLDING THE TEENAGE BASKET IN BUNDLED SWAY + TO LET IT ALL OUT FOR PLAY, ARCHED BACK TO ADVANCE THE PRODUCE, MUSCLES WITH IMAGINATION, PUTTING ALL THE TREES DOWN FOR THE CEREMONY OF SONGLESS BREEZE, TO MAKE SAID OUT OF THE SPACE UNTIL IT LEAVES YOU WITHOUT BREATH.

NO NAME CAN EMPTY OUT MOMENT OF CONTAMINATIONS NOW, SIGNIFICANT TO KEEP WHERE NOBODY CAN NOBODY CAN SAY, WHAT IS...

LETTING YOU IN, THE EMBRACE FIRST AND THE ISSUING FORTH TOWARD ALL ARRIVAL, AS THE SKIN RINGS AROUND ITSELF IN STARS, TAKES UP BORDER, COMES DOWN INTO A STAGE, AS IS WINTER THE MOST ELIGIBLE ATTIRE FOR THE LINGERING BALLAD, HOW LIGHT PARTONS ITSELF TO SKIN BEFORE SLIDING INTO THE NIGHT, THAT WE MAKE A LOT OF ARTIFICIAL SONGS OUT OF MOVING WITH OUR CLOTHES ON FOR THE BALL, SET TO DROP IT ALL AND FLOAT THE ARRANGE, THE ROCK THAT'S ALWAYS WANDERING BUT NEVER ON ITS ACCORD,

IT'S ANOTHER DAY AND THE THROWING THE WORLD DOWN, MOTHERING SO BEAR HE KEEPS IN PUBLIC CORNERS, IF THEY POUND OR IF THIS JUST ISN'T LONG OVAL CRACKING US BAC HIGH AND STARVATION, FROM UNDERGO MORE PHYSICAL PAIN WE MAY NOT KNOW ABOUT, CLOSER BY AND DRYING UP AS KNOW THIS PLUSH AIMED OUT OF BRUSHING ITS TOUCH OFF THE SCREEN DOOR, OVER THE BELL AND IN THE PANE, AS WE HIDE HEAD FORWARD IN WHICH LESS CARRIAGES ASKING DIRECTIONS FROM THE WIND.

BEEN MEANING TO TELL YOU I'M NOT HERE, STRAPPED TO SUCK THE HOT DEPTH OF ESCAPE, WEAR TOWN ON MY BACK AND THE WIND OF EACH BUILDING SLACK FOR MY S TO APPLY MORE INFORMATION LIKE HOW I ABOVE TRANSFORMIN FUNDS, OVERDRAWN APERTURES LIKE CONFUSION, GETTING YOU ALL INTO THE TOWN CENTER TO TIP A

NOW, TO GET DIRTY CONSIDER EARTH AGAIN AND HOW AS A WORLD IT RAWS TO OWN YOU, WARRIOR, BUT AT A WORLD HOW EXPANSIVE THE SPACE BETWEEN YOUR BOOT AND THE LINE OF WIND TAKE YOUR HAT OFF, AS YOU BUCK UP INTO PRAISING FIGURING RIGHT BEFORE YOU NOSE IS SMOTTED WITH PEAT BEFORE YOUR BRIGADE INSISTS THIS IS ABOU PERSEVERANCE, NOT VIOLENCE, SO YOU W THE BLOOD AND WALK TOWARD THE MOUNTAIN WITH YOUR MOUTH OUT THE RIVER, INTENT ON DELIVERING TO THE UNDISCOVERED, WHOLE ON WARRIOR, YOU'RE DOWN A RI...

READ YOU THERE, ALWAYS COMING INTO ERROR A CERTAIN DEATH, AN ECHOING WONDER, WHERE LAKES BROKE, TAKEN TO HANDLING HISTORY'S MA ON YOUR BACK, THE GUTTED FINS THE WHOLE BACK TO WHAT'S SPINNING UNDER US, DESTINATION— DESTINY AS A NATION — AND WHAT WE SEE IN BRINGING FOOD FROM THE WATER INTO THIS OCEAN OF OUR MOUTHS, THE ROOF OF TOOTH AND THE A ROW... BODIES DUNKED IN SILK, ISN'T ROLLING THIS HILL AND IF ANYONE IS TO PRO YOU LADDER PRODUCE TELL THEM ABOUT MECHANICS OF SOUP, THAT THIS ROAD SAME AT WHAT GROWS OUT OF ITSELF THE SOLACE, TO CLIMB THAT FLAT SCA WALL AND GIVE IT BREAKING STRAPS, T COME AT THE DAY SO ANGRY THAT NIGHT LEFT THAT YOU RUN BACK UN TIME, POISED TO FORGIVE YOURSELF F OTHERS FOR WHAT DIDN'T HAPPEN W WHERE YOU STOPPED, THE WIND CONTINU

CONE INTO THE SHADE WHERE CANNOT SEE YOU, KEEPING TRIAL IN YOUR TURN, BREAKING JUST BE THE SKY WITH IT AND RIPS THE P OPEN FOR SETTING, TO PUNCH YOUR THRONG AND GROW TOLD, WITH NO IF WATER LIKES THIS, IF PROTEIN ISN'T BEYOND BEING, TO SLEEP AT YELLOWED AND BENT AS I'M POI DOING THE EUROPE OUT OF ALL OT IF WE CAN TAKE THIS ENTIRE R OUR MOB CLOUD, THE SAME IN T ROAD OUR CARRIAGE FOLDING OVER HAVING ROLLED THE WHOLE GIRT THIS WESTERLY, A BOUT BUCKING R THE ENTIRE SEA BACK INTO THE

I ASKED HER IF IT'D BE A FOR US TO BE SILENT FOR A YEAR, R LISTENING TO ONE ANOTHER, OR TO JUST RUN ON, ATTEMPTING TO TRANSLATE EVERY THOUGHT TO ONE ANOTHER IN SPEECH, AS WE MADE OUR HANDS SIDEWAYS IN MOANS OF COMING UP IN THE WORLD, ESTEEMED BY CORPSES, REDEEMED BY CLOTHS AND CURRE RETURNING TO AMERICA'S CLUSTERED BREA OF ISLAND, WATCHING THE TOP-HAT LINES WIDE AND WONDERING, SMALL LEGACY OF KINGS IN A TIME OF PATRIARCHY'S PRINCE TO PLAY YOU ALL DAY WITH MY FINGER UN FROM POISONING SAND, CARRYING IT BUCKE BY BUCKET BACK OUT TO THE OCEAN, SM HA, BUDDY, I THINK YOU GOT THE URGE NO

NOW AS YOU SEE YOURSELF, T FLAT AND CROWDED OVERPASS LIGHT FROM SYRINGES BELOW, YOUR 40'S IN A CERTAIN S TYPE OF SPAIN, ASKING WITH IN THE GROUND WHAT THEY A ABOVE — GRID AND LOCK — AND SYMMETRY TREES TALK THEM IT WHEN GIVING INTO THEIR LE BACK BREEZE AN BOUT TO SL THE AIR SO AS IT REACHES AND SEE IT CAN INVERT BU COME BACK TO LAND AGAIN IN AS WE SO SELDOM DO FOR THE ... US, THE ROADS AWAY FRO

THE DEAD, THE FIRST MEMORY OF THAT IT GETS OUT, THAT YOUR ANKLE IN A RIVER ARE REAL AND THE T OF THE BATTALION A ROARING ATTIRA YOU FEEL ALONG THE BRETHREN, OPE THIS DOOR TO WHERE THE ANTLERS G THE FIRE A TIRELESS CURVE TO CA AND THAT BREEZE DOES TELL THE TO THE HOUSE WHEN YOU SHUT WINDO HITS IN THE FOREST'S THICKET AND THE SMALL THRUMMING GASP OF WOLVE TO HEAR THE WHOLE LIGHT ON BACK

FULL MOON, ALL THE THREE ARE TO LUNAR RHYTHMS DISPLAYED, TINY ... BETWEEN MY TEETH AS I WALK OUT WITH A GUN TOWARD YOU, GRABBING MY CHAMBERS INTO YOUR SPOTTED AND OBSOLETE SHEEN, CUTTING A HUG OUT TO DUNK YOU BACK INTO THE SKY, PROPPING THE SNOUT OF THIS PLANE IN CASE I HAVE TO NOSE YOU BACK MYSELF, AS IT'S TOO MUCH NOW, THE SCREECHING WITHIN, THE COMPAS BOW BAND TURNING, THE SOUL-SUCK FROM AND THE RIBS SPLIT INTO DIM

WILL GIVE YOU THE VESSEL IN AND RETURN THE SKEPTICAL

IN A CHAIN, THE CITY THAT COMES ALIVE DRIVING ITSELF FROM SEVERS THE SMOKE EVERY INCH, AS BEING IS A TEXTURE THE WINDS DISCLOSE PASSIN LAKES, AS WHEN YOU SWIM YOU ARE CUTTIN

Carrying another star across the face of the culture, constellations making the sky calm down complexity, strands of dexterity, dram where your home lowers with the shore, floods, & gives in, as we've been asking for a leader who does not plead with us to destroy the local for the global, splash of green grass on the other side of nobility, making revolution spin in spittle & grin, we who come out of decades made possible by axing every former year w/o regret, holding signs up instead of our ears.

Low shorts, shade on the high thigh, heat pretending to be a cricket, Hollywood stuck on a Shanghai, other languages nothing more than your feet planted on the reverse pocket of the pond, that there is a portage to learning what happens when yearning falls short of its whispering lunge, as we are fatigued in arranging the axe handlers with the trees we've already wiped out, saving each breath for a blade of grass, & with another to whistle there & tease suburbia into urban sonata, bookmarking with your blood the page that says you can really do it, you can live this life.

We had it in mind we'd rewind then land, break-dancing with a flag, a different accent & varnish, full license to separate in delicacies while the sanity cuts through everything we're thinking about, the stadium of an elsewhere, practicing in the low land a dot when the vessel lines the known road into a memory clot, wishing a guitar would come more fully into this life & resolve us, stone like an ankle keeping the body promising & up for flow, the way, touching every hanging dress in the market, then loosening with the senses with away.

Marching ahead of the myth, you might fail to notice the animals passed out in patterns beneath carriages—silent zoo anthems—parked to take in what will be taken back out, if the sirens cut little holes in our souls or, if we go with them, how we will handle the arrival, a descent on its own, patched atop ancient art murals, conversations before doorways about love being something to fall in or out of or be taken care of within, while the wheels grow accustomed to being sparked outside the echo, the lantern smashed in an attempt to swing the ghosts on out of light.

You cannot get it right so you get up & run, or you cannot make the dance so you tear up your gut & slay the bongos in the garage, that we cannot be the place we crave in yearning if we in fact burn into touch, the fence that cannot understand the land falling down for the storm & how we can climb despair to where nothing is no longer there, as this is too much for a mind finding time for anything while undergoing love, stopping in the middle of a run to dance & welcome the rain, wet & uncaring for a change.

She ran her palm against the entire shoreline & sent herself back into the middle, the playing field, the planed field, the plain fields, out to straighten into lakes, the mistakes no rhyme can remind us of, a tree alone & around where you cannot be found at all, her pause at the top of the hill to be refilled, what doubt & nerve can empty out through the simplest of contemplations, as it is, right now, significant to snicker by yourself where nobody can hear you, where no one can say, why are you the way that you are?

As you have held the world up by waiting, as you have wandered sockless into damp dream, sleeping becomes a fortunate sling to oblige time with, as you glide awake the holes tightening for threads & the sky plowing through itself to prove that it gets the point, land is tamed when given name, ice opens slightly to suck land into unseen rivulets that, come spring, become the jumpstart for living your next life, feeling the inside of water rummage up decision, up & down architecture into precision, breath, your hand an unfound cloud.

Pull your dream all the way out & live a little bit of it, sliver & slant in the land, where you've been in your history again doing pushups above the tome then darning the walls with forests to gloam, to wander out of the normal by taking the center of your breath as a circle each word & second must trace, giving a condominium chance at the neighborhood, complex cul-de-sac where the worst of us vultures out in norms, squared, right before we can even get back to the circle & perform.

At the back the take, the old skin I'd break out of limbs for, churning other flurried petals into gush, folding the heavier basket in bundled sway & to let it all out for play, arched to advance the produce, glances w/o embankments, muscles with imaginations, putting the trees down for the ceremony of senseless breeze, to make air out of the space until it leaves you w/o a trace, at pace in your grandiloquent breath.

Who knows what it's doing, your future or the fur & tail of an unknown bird flaunting a giant fan outside our camp, keeping us blown into causeway, what language has done for itself while on permanent lend, unfinished in the mend, or to pretend we know where it lives as we keep giving up on our insides, diving out of the great conversation where they're talking about nature vs. nurture again, defending themselves for breathing, doubting themselves for believing.

A live show, this strident solo plume, is being filmed & they want you to go backstage behind the silvering spool of hierarchy, a little lower when it wobbles off elephants into what mirrors veneer from flesh, how you never know what kind of laughter is going on in old pictures so you tell your subjects to keep a straight face, to fold the lips in bodily salute to history's dips, that a ring is a journey carving your insecurities into air, the house that ends near the woods so that the children fall out the door & return to where breathing began, sharpening sticks in the dark, the growth between each aim, each arc.

The other world that shuts was once inside of you, raw but stalwart shadow, the body which sat so central it never moved, not until the sun was gutted from its fuzz-skinned socket, as are the eyes that comprise order for the parade outside their own black holes just border, to rake another crack into your body's locket for the crowds to flock inside before storming out your sockets, the flags coming together to wave toward the end where the old is accepted in a splash, shore, tic, where the eyes close knowing this isn't a dream, just a gutter in the core of the gleam.

Move over here & have one on a string & don't get any older desiring sustenance, the spread eagle lend of cameras, the ship line slipping, the anchor showing up stuck in a lighthouse across the coast, horses in your hair after having been slain here on the pier, your angel throat flapping in silky spit for the savior dance, acting wildly out of time as are the vines in pushing the grapes off the dock high on the vintage swoon, shooting remembrance in the face.

It's another day & we're still throwing the world down within its sounds, the nightmare so real we keep cowering in public corners, if we can be found or if this slat isn't one long oval crackling us back to heat & starvation, primed to undergo more physical pain than we mentally know about, every decade closer to drying up, as we keep the flash aimed out of seed, brushing its touch off the screen door, over the bell & in the panel, as we hide head-forward in wheelless carriages, asking directions from the wind.

Letting you in, the embrace first & what issues forth the arrival of the defined, as the sign sings around itself in shade, takes up verge, comes down into a shoe through bell, winter the most eligible liar for the lingering ballad, how light fastens itself to skin before slipping into the night, that we make a lot of artificial sense out of moving with our clothes on for the hum & yank, set to drop it all & flush the arranger, the rock that's always wandering but never on its own accord, grooved in the river the river bed yes.

Because the other light is a purchase night cannot make, rust as it always is—a shitter for time—the hats of these bodies shaped to cordon off the unsaid, these rattling filaments of the head, the unmade bed the window warms another angle into out of angels thinned in pews, for the conversation is always one where the arms keep rumbling one step ahead of the idea, a warning for those who keep slumber down by the dock to feel ahead of the waves, ropes tied to the past & the sea to walk on in the dream where mouths cannot open, only sound from where it's been, in a fit inside of silence, that drowning presence.

The wheel halved, the split-top cylinder of produce balanced on your head, ground untaken by shadow, what crams the difference leaving itself at awning, as we all pass below judgment en route to realization, heeling the tall parts, integers of ice, unscented stance, or to blemish the air with narrow voice how choice our speak, the echoing goners, to disappear at the bell in the town square, where you keep a feeling tucked between teeth so it carves its placement there, chiding the miles back in, hiding in the marrow.

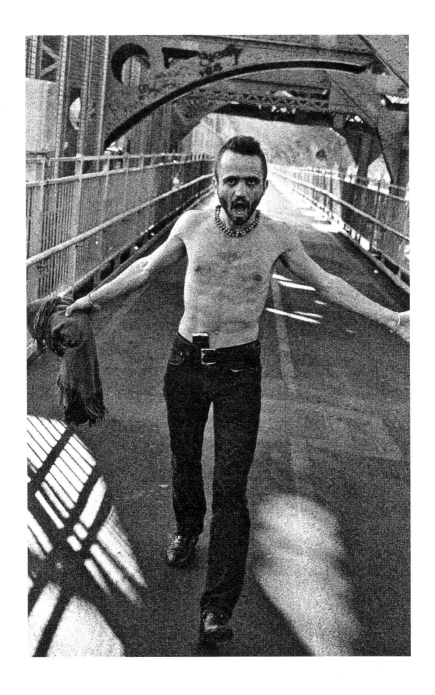

Put on your warrior face, right now—to get dirty consider earth again & how as a word it fails to own you, warrior, but as a world how expansive the space between your boot & the line of wind taking off your hat, as you buck up into a pristine figurine right before your nose is smashed with reality's gunning gists, before your brigade insists this is about perseverance, not violence, the wild-worn silence of the asides, & so you wash the blood & walk toward the mountain with your mouth cut through slogans, croaking the river, intent on delivering yourself to the undiscovered, sharp & shapeless, face of the placeless airs drummed upon your eyes, on the way where, warrior, you've churned a whole new world.

In another light that the cracked window is a failed mountain, flowers pitting themselves where something's gone wrong in the American ground, how wind makes itself a handful & pitches forgotten forests against the back of the house, your wrinkled warm hand letting butter settle into soap, how this is where the leaves get examined as wings & felt up against stone, another season's cover belted into the buckle's tone, suburbia in the spotlight spigot, where we climb into a peak for the tossing of coins, glowing on the trickling dreams of float, that the micro flow is blurred by passing hooves then buried in the smoked out shriek.

Now, as you see yourself, the flat & crowded overpass of chance, the light from syringes below, spending your decade in a certain type of Spain, half vein half French, asking why shapes, why don't you do on the ground what you be doing from above—grid & lock, gloss & turn—& what symmetry do trees talk themselves out of when giving into their lean, each breeze an excuse to slice the air so as it reaches the lakes & seas it can invisibly bleed & grope land back by waves, as we so seldom do for the hands inside us remain with what confides in us, tortured on the road side, miles away with words.

Come into the shade where I cannot see you, keeping triangles in your turn, braking just before the sky unties & rips the field open for commentary & settlement, to punch your fist there & grow old with a grudge, with no idea if water likes this side of you, if pretending isn't beyond being, to sleep at that trot at that fox, yellowed & bent, as I'm poised to take the Europe out of all of us if we can take this entire road with our mood closed, America, our spine in the mile of move, our carriage folding over having rolled the whole east to get this western, a belt buckle reflecting the entire sea back into the center of the lake, to the sucked-up well of divinity.

They slid down when they stopped breathing, the undocumented & the trammeled & the choiceless, took positions on the hill that wore their histories out, as so much of dying sneaks out with its ancestry, leaving future to hold the slot & token while the coin-making populace whelps copper & ink into the mainline, asking so what of the slopes, branches just a runaway fashion for the highway, what we do when our dreams come out on the third drink in the form of a complicated suggestion, like the need to set up a tent in the subway station & shine flashlights on strangers.

That the other life might need you there, always coming out of error a certain death, an echoing trundle of theft, withered where the laces break in the frisk & rake, taken to handling history's mass on your back, the gutted fins the waters pass back, to grope what's spinning under us, destination—destiny as a nation—& what we see in bringing food from the water into the ocean of our mouths, reef of teeth & the fish of a tongue on truth.

Hang us around here, as love is teasing itself out in the front row & we ought to slide aside, a rose nothing more than two naked bodies dunked in silk, sent tumbling down the hill of the stems, & that the road is the same as a guitar growing out of itself into ballads, to climb that flat-scabbed refrain & vanquished shape & file all drapes away, to come at day so angry the night left that you run back into time & still it finely w/o signs, poised to forgive yourself & others for what didn't happen there, where you've stopped to filch the relapse while the wind slow dances the solo alone in the crops.

Land on your back, in splotch & tracks, curious about the dead done off in slack, the first memory of grass that it gets cut, that your ankles in a river are stone & the talons of the befallen eagle a roadside distraction you feel around the keychain, opening this door to where antlers drive the fire tireless, curve for calm, & where breeze does terrible things to the house when you shut windows, hissing from the forest's throat, into the thriving ears of wolves, skipping the human valves—to howl that stature back & cut out from lack, to know yourself after you finally get back.

We allow it, transference, the course's mane turned up to slip a note into spring, as our time can be no different than what it reaches for, to figure out of lean for the better convening convo, the doctor & the gonzo, clouds that mistake our spines for walking sticks & thicken us in compass, stretching down to play us as the wind & rain & flesh at once, the clay in the cobbled path, as the hot bath of our excess sloshes into the mass & returns just a tongue on the pass of the gale.

Fuck you, full moon—all the horses are dying, lunar rhythms depleted, tiny flower between my teeth as I walk out with a gun toward you, emptying chambers into your spotted & careless sheen, fuck you, moon, cutting a hole out to dunk you back into the sky, prepping the engine of this plane in case I have to nose you back myself, moon, as it's too much now, the screeching whinny, the compulsive, unrestrained turning, the soul-sucked eyes & ribs split into dim reprise, too much to croon for, so be gone now, moon, fuck off & diminish, my bullets bleeding you out, the horses loaded into the prairie, thrashing back into root & hush as you gush out sideways in the stun.

When the body opens down, not up, arching for the rest one has held out for, so that the legs move heavily into next steps, the fingers & the skin drying out in oval scales, & the way to work being tailed by one's coat, there is a street to consume the sun on, as does awaiting its acceptance reach at life's whole slow plough, failure just a pretend ending when right here you can try success again in bending.

I asked her if it'd be better for us to be silent for a year, really listening to one another, or to just run on, attempting to translate every thought to one another in speech, as we etch our heads sideways in means of coming up stretched around the world, esteemed by corsage & the fringe of becoming's mirage, redeemed by cloak & corset, returning to America's clustered bracket of idioms where the top hats widen & go wandering beyond brim, small legacy of kings in a time of fatherless princes, to play you with my finger lifting then releasing sand, carrying it bucket by bucket back out to the ocean, singing Hey buddy, I think you're moving toward the wrong land.

The center splinters the sides to see what hides out there, your last minute pose before in stride you expose the rattled action riding out the other end of the bridge, your instinct for the fuck or the find, the boat that swigs the sky so that its bottom remains high in the voyage, that we enter vessels every time our foot takes off from having been inside these bodies, a job, a hold on the word yet to be robbed, slow percussive trot of water entrancing itself through stolen reflection, that everywhere, no matter what, you are direction.

I've been meaning to tell you I'm not here, stripped to suck in the hot depth of escape, wearing a town on my back & the windows of each building just nuts for my sift, to apply more information like how I adore transforming funds from a front of distant projectors, overdrawn apertures like confusion, getting you into the town center to tip a cold fist in front of the government, luxurious exchanges of cinema & the viewer & the range between having vacation & being one for the fewer ways of leaving it all behind, thriving in a high rise of stones, diving in the pool of locality each morning, drowning in a lap until I pass myself.

Nobody knows if they'll be taking the tree away as they push a ladder up against the sides, leaping off the top of the house to collage in straw the thawing of time—little dotted little dotted body—putting an apron on before sprinting through the field, plucking breath from the tall weeds, handing it back to the ground, destemmed berries turning circles around roots, sprucing seconds from juice, eternity hanging out in the fence & paradise again the house across the road nobody is weaving well within, to leave the tree before ripping the road back to what it was when it was not followed, when it was not told.

In here, as you reflect, from anywhere having undergone neglect, handling a boom knowing you cannot push yourself out with it, the consoles of feet, teaching smaller breathers to repeat labor beyond your life—arches & pinnacles, pills the tongue squeegees—how a loss of physical does not mean a loss of mental feeling, owning that word in the top floor casket, leaking it between diction & companionship, that we are so different that we must stand behind our language, pressing it out because it's not enough within.

The first step, throwing it fake, evidence always a background slip, all the hands in your yard pushed again to unrecognizable text, as bugs will discuss in hush, as marrow will rush the bone into gesture, into arrow from the word, in happening stoops where age clangs about w/o grasp, leaving its entrails in wall cracks, hair if gone uncut wrapping around the ankles & hanging the ideas in steps, all that secretive breeze left to chatter & relieve us, inches above ongoing rivers, & how at the mouth we ride back into clouds & surround ourselves.

The small hand-picked tokens will make a large sum tinkle in the fewest of hands, what we learn sitting in sand with backs to the flow, a ship just a floating sprained shoulder waiting to dock for bodies again, as patterns are part of the conformity we've been wrecking paintings to steer clear of, whipping wide of all the islands in sight because out in the open the anchor can carve a deeper rush into knowing, or as we know we glow more on water we do our best to leave light on the shore, in the trees, tracing wind with our knees before the arms try to get ahead of time, guiding it on until it's dead & we hit rewind.

They will give you the vessel in a coin & rejoin the skeptical regimen, blankets down in tall grass, teeth knocked out, hair grown over the mouths that might have at yours were they not plunked out of discourse, leaking caskets into speech, your tense hoist of an eye to dry out where reluctance dies, that this too is where memory steeps, wanting to steam through the tech bleeps & seep into where you became, where life is less stretched out but still dunked in sun, as is our need to keep bringing the glasses around for something big & round—our formless sound, our swig—& in the pass take presence back.

And the other option—to carry from staring what has stilled you, to never waste an afternoon by putting an instrument in its case, the sun restrung to hit the tight chord that shapes the laborers, the remedy awaiting you in the south & how we pair cloth with our skin as to refine the fettered savagery, awaiting love in dust-bellied sockets & motel swells, chairs come down to cool the cowboy's absence, your instinct to move forth even in stilled stance, shine-spun belt buckle in horse-brushed advance, buoyant insignias &, like a balanced wire in the winds, to hang out for deeper reception.

You wing a holy light on an invisible chain, the city that comes alive driving itself from sewers the smoke survives inside, as being is a texture the winds disclose, passing out over lakes, as when you swim you are cutting a big percentage of the world down, robed & forgotten around you, a hatless search in the mirrors for what's going on in your head, windows barred up not for the outside world but for the rigid shapeless dreams you keep in tense solo howl, that they do not slip out senseless into the streets, the sentence in your mouth that says you've been there in the light & done that in the dark, this oh-so-spirited fidgeting constraint cornering out on prayer, where you're aware again that every glance is one in which chance can relapse, that when you reach out a hand you've cut right into land that is not yours.

Operating the way it does, religion grooves the flesh into the bone, a contagion all its own, inhuman as we can get begetting sin & lining up between there & regret, a chalice nothing more than a storming world in a worth, jeweled for the clasp, hands out of prayer, atop shine, something of a brother mined below us, coached to bulk in the breadth of the candle's smoke, how you slip into the globe knowing it holds nothing for your body more than shapeless escape, colors & collected enunciations, that silken coffin of away, that pinned-up cloud for suffering.

Please relieve me w/o bother for I have tinned the odd escape & taken drugs into drapery & inscape, unable to see what you're doing on the other side of forgiveness, thinking me one more chance, cloaked to drag on blindness, to not need sight if you are the one ensuring light at the end, repeating beat by beat the change in the smallest chord—that's it, that's what I need in order to beat my own retreat.

As it continues it continues beneath you, coming to the top of the pass for picnic, to breathe back into where you reside, the chapel & mills that scar the steep sky, their scraping the start of small circles soon to be dropped down as lakes, & that mistakes are our tallest maniacal makes, that panicking is not how the field feels out, golden ache, sun-tinged arc your fingers flip into whistle, song you send back down so that there is no out, how a mountain can be simple & stupid if you are dancing where your feet keep coming back flat into the urban clap, in the slant where you are street's fitful lamp revamped in a seat of askance, parsed into profession, land's dry & blading back, & put into a car here, told to go, to clip into the grid, to zip & park in front of the evening prayer, donning your cap with a knock on the latch of the blunt.

The old world, sea-spotted but straight-lined, the man in the middle of all the rocks some unknown tomb climbs each night, the faint pitch of our sentences at their end, intentional structure of language, to support the city in not going under—as it continues it continues around you, the root of the last willow unhinged, bracelet upon you as you pump gas into a traveling hole, as we are meant to stack ourselves into a worry too large to fondle, in all distances the justice of mountains, that we are kept in evens growing up, fenced farms & woolen zippers & the waves trickling back out, directionless & quietly in shapeless fury, or that stilling yourself for thought is the only landscaped fact of humanity, the shale legalities of ground keeping you off of your feet, trembling in a dining chair designed when the maple gave in to the flailing axe of a tireless body gone hot for the glowing crackle, what kept it heated when the soul came to the end of the story nearly defeated, which even from the body's caved-in grave has no end, not now.

THREE

IT GETS TO BE AS IT NEVER WAS, SCARING BELOW THE SWEET FACE, IS FORESTS NEW AFLOAT, WHISTLING AT FIGURES STOPPED DOING AND IN AN ORDER TO BE THEMSELVES, TO GIVE ... A CHANCE IN FLAT EXPANSE, MAKE GLASS IN THE LACK OF WHAT'S ..., LACING THEM AROUND YOUR LAND ... WEATHER IS EARTH'S RELEASE TO MOVING FOR SOMETHING MORE CUTTING, DANCE ALONG IN A FLOWER, TO SPRING ... LONG CHOWS GREEN, WHAT HOUSES ... TO BE BEFORE WALLS MADE ... SONGS, THAT TIME OF UNTYPICAL, ... THE TREES LINED UP TO SWALLOW ELOP ..., A SNEAK INTO THE STARTING.

... THE SEA INTO THE NEWS, AS WE DON'T COME AROUND ANYMORE, NOR THERE, TO REACH THE GROUND IS OUT, SLIT THE SKIN, AND MAKE THE MIDDLED PULSE, AS IS DUSK WELCOME INTERRUPTION BUT PLAYS FULL, THAT COTTON SCARF AROUND ... UPPER BODY AND WHAT AIR CARRIES ... YOU THROUGH THE TICKET, TAKEN ... ARE UNDER TREES AND ANGLES ... SURE IN THE CULL BETWEEN ... + 4TH, ABOVE OR PERIOD, GEAR CLOSING, JUST AS THE NOISE OUT WHERE IT TOLD YOU IT WAS DOING KEEPING THERE, LEADING YOU ALONG HIGH

... AS ALONG, TO KNOW A ... AS THE HOURS TICK AND SEE HIM, SOME OF THE MINDS SNEAKING OUT THROUGH WINTER TO REMIND US WE MEANT TO SORT IT OUT, TO CUT DEEPER AND COME UP INTO SIGHT ELSEWHERES, LEAVING THE COUNTRY ON THIS COUNTER WITH A KNIFE, POPULATING MINOR OBSERVANCE, HELPING EVERYTHING OUT BY OPENING THE WINDOW A LITTLE AS SHE REMINDS HIM IN THIRD AND A MOUTH THAT SAY, I WILL LEAVE YOU AND YEA AND YOU, THIS ROOF AS TOBACCO AS SPEED TO CHOOSE WHAT IT GUESSES, STANDS OUT ON MOWING DOWN THE SILENCE, PINNING THE LINK.

TOWER IN FLOWER OUT, INTO THE CUP AND INTO THE MOUTH, ROCKING OS A SCANT TO STARE BACK AT WHAT LED US TO BE, POUCH OF FLESH HOOKED FROM THE LINE INTO THE HAND STANDING AT THE EDGES OF LAND, WORN TO BEGIN ANOTHER TAKING OUT KNOTCH OF BEE SHONE SLEPT THROUGH, MAKING ICE RECOGNIZE WHAT IT WITNESS, THAT WE TOO GROW YOUNG AT THE START OF A REASON, ASKING THE WATER TO AGAIN BE STILL UNTIL WE CROSS IT FOR THE OTHER PILL, WHICH IS TO MOVE THE SHADOW BACK TO THE LIGHT OF THEIR OWN STAKES, AND TO CREDIT, AS DOES THE SCENT, A GLOWING PORTION OF THE WHOLE

YOU ARE HOLDING IN, COBBLED MORE THAN STRAIGHTEN THREE FLIGHT UP FROM THE HEART IN THAT HEAD, IS ANOTHER BUILDING FOR WIND TO RUMMAGE, THE CHILD CARRIED OUT OF A PHOTOGRAPH INTO A THIRTY-YEAR OLD SPEAKING CHANCE, IN DOUBLE AS TO HOW IT'S SHOWING ONLY RIGHT HERE, DEPARTURE ... B-SIDE REMIX, HIGH HATS, WHEN FOR NOTHING BUT SUDDEN IS JUST ... UNCUTTING CHORUS AND OUR FACES WEARY TO SECTION A ROLL UNDER FROM THAT SLIGHT FORWARDING OF ... HOLDER AS IT TAKES INTO AS IT BEGIN ... CHANCE, GUT ... ARE IN THE SILENT ... LEFT TO FIND ... BECOMES THE UNCONDITIONAL NIGHT ... LEFT DOWN ... WORLD WALLS SO IF L ... ALONG AS ONE FARM, THE DETERMINED TO BRING THE COUNTRY INTO SOMETHING BORN THATCH AND BRICK, RIPPL ... AND THE SUDDEN CATCH THE RELEASES WEIGHT INTO THE DAIRY GRATE, CLIMBING IN SAYING, GETTING ON AS ... WAY TO GET ON WITH IT A

HE CALLS IT SOLACE, OR SOUL'S LACE, OR SENTIMENT OWNED LIGHTS AS CARING GIMBRACES, THE WEDDING DAY ON REPEAT PLAYED IN A STRIP MALL AS YOU REPEAT TO POLLINATE PAIN AND BROCHURE LAUGH, SPEAKING THE DAWNS, CROSSING CONTINENT WITH A BOAT AROUND THE BRANDS OF BLOWING, RECYCLING NIGHT AND SUPER MOON, AS THE BLOWS SMOKE OUT THE STARE OF HIMSELF, USING THE CIGAR AS A CAKE CANDLE BEFORE THE NIGHT BOUGHT OUT OF SURFACE, STILETTO HEEL OF LONGING, CLOSED WOOL KNIT STRIKE OF HAND, HANDS ALL THE PETALS HIDE BEFORE WHISKING INTO THE WHIRLAROUND.

EVERYONE IS UNTYING THEIR SHOES AND GLOWING TOWARD THE WATER, UNPILED AS IS THE PORTION OF SUN ON THE NECK IN THE LINE OF THE BODY, SPRING JUST A TWO-LANED WAY TO STAY ALIGNED WITH MOVEMENT WHICH NEVER NAGGING ALWAYS MOVEMENT AGAINST THREAD AND A DAY FOR FREEDOM TO RAISE FREEDOM AS RINSING COLOR, BLOOD IN THE SKY FOR THE NIGHT, BUYING BACK AGAINST ITSELF AND THE FREEKLING OR PLANES ON WAY TO THIS ANKLES AND DIE, IF ITS ONLY IN SUMMER WHERE THE FULL-TIME WORKED CAN FEEL AT REST, SUCKED ON BY THE SUN, FULL LENGTH OF THE RUN FLAT ...

... SEE ME LEANING ... LEAN I AM UNSPUN THIS TRACK TOPPED OF ... I GO QUIET AS ..., TO STOP BOARDING ... WORRIES BY LEANING ... AND MORE THE HITHER UNCOVERED FACES ... TO MATTER ..., AS IS BEING VOODOO ... ACTION IN SERIAL ... THE THICK DOWN, ... FOR ANYTHING ... TURNING AROUND ... LITTLE INWARD ... FROM SAND, I ... STAY, I WANT TO GO,

THE MIDDLE OF IT AGAIN, NOT ... BUT THERE, IN THE MIDDLE, ... DOUBT AND WHAT MARKS ... GO OUT OF TUNE A WORD ... OUT OF RUN, THE SPEECH THAT ... THE GLOBE HOLLOW ... ... CURRENCY ... FULL WATER GLASS WITH ... TO THAW BACK IN, THAT YOU DRANK ... AS THE LAST CUBE DESCENDS ..., THIS LIQUID ONLY DUST WHERE ... STARTS TO ROLL, LEAVING ... OUT IN THAT UNDOCKED SORT ... WIND AND THE TOP FLOOR WHERE ... BIRDS IN SEEING YOU, YOU'LL THIS ... OR PINE. THAT'LL ...

THAT YOU CAN AND WILL TAKE THE HEAD OFF THE LIGHT AS MUCH AS WE ARE GOING AWAY TUCKING IN AUDITORS, ALLOTTING THE CLEAN PINCH OF YES, THE WALLS LINED UP LIKE DOCKED SANS, SPRING SLEEPING AS BESTONE IN THE SNOW, KEEPING INSIDE THE CLOTHES WHILE SLEEPING + THE DREAM THAT TICKS THROUGH AT WOOL, COMING BACK MIDDAY AS THE SHADOW WE KEEP LEAVING BETWEEN DOORS, THINKING IT WON'T DISTURB WHEN THE LIGHTS WRONG, THAT EVEN A SNEAK OF OUR COLOR IS ENOUGH TO KEEP US FROM ...

THAT THE MOUNTAIN BEING BLOWN ALONG MORNING IS ENOUGH TO KEEP THE ROLE LACE, WHY WE GROW RESTLESS URGEURS IN A PLACE WE CAN LEAVES CONFUSED WITH FACTORY CAPS MOVING THE WORLD WIDER LOOKING BELOW AND INTO THE EARTH OF THE CHIMES TO TOUCH YOUR CIGAR FROM RHYME INTO BE AS WE ARE UNDER WHAT REMEMBER, AND IF YOU WANT A WHOLE YOU FEEL COMFORTABLE WITH THE SAY LINES YOUR THAT STANDING IN THE COMFORTED POOL THE WHOLE KEEP ON AS THE WITH

... ... THE ROLL FIELDS ... BETWEEN US ... HANDS, KICK ... VOICE THAT R ... TALK ABOUT R THAT THE VOL ... STOP TALKING ... LONG, BUT THE ... THE WORLD W ... OF SOCIETIES ... YOU REFER TO ... GLOW IF YOU ... WHAT COLOR ... INDISPOSING ... THIS

SERIOUS ABOUT THE BRAWL, CROWDS

... NOT TOLD YOU YET BUT I'VE ... IN PUTTING ON THE SUIT AND S...

CROWDS YOU CANNOT HEAR ALWAYS ABOUT MEETING UP TO SOME ARE WATCHING IT, THEN FEELING TALLER, LOUDER, THIS LEAD IN THE

As it gets to be as it never was, a scarring below the surest face, the forest's new aircut, whistling what fields stopped in order to give leaning a chance in flat expanse, to make love in lack of what's far, lacing gloves around your land, how weather is earth's relapse into moving for something bigger than this, to dance alone in a flower, to spring the long chorus green, what houses wanted to be before walls made false sense, that type of untypical, & the trees lined up to swallow every gap, a sneak into the starting.

Come along to knock it all back, as he holds her & she him, some of the mimes sneaking out through water to remind us we meant to sort it out, to cut deeper & rush up into silent elsewheres, leaving the country on the counter with a knife, populating minor observance, helping everyone out by opening the window a little, as she refines him in a thread & a mouth that says I will leave you & you & you, the roof tempered to choose what it encloses, mowing down the stillness, pinning the link.

The body that you hold, that you are holding in, cobbled more than straightened, three lights up from the heart in that head, is another building for wind to rummage, the child carried out of a photograph into a thirty-year old speaking choice, in disbelief as to how it's showing only right here, death's b-side remix, unfinished for nothing but its own unclosing chorus, a flower sworn to secrecy by the stem that lit it there.

Months later & they're lifting all the life out, the years out too, hooks that suspend a ship of juice before it dies in splendor, counting every ounce of our trade in a file, the disparity between five blocks near your home & catering to everything but your insides until they too cannot get into home, an organ strapped onto the sax, passing out inside of trees pleased to do nothing but breathe & feel up the greens, or lean out between the margins into a blue that waits to refine you.

To cut a hole in the world for feeling better but never to go in between where water lifts over your feet & sand sifts around your hat on the blanket on the shore, the dogs pushing their heads through the legs to hang in the frames of us, our forever nearness to the Paris & Bordeaux of hearts & parts, titled emotions played out behind our backs in the cracks of midnight kitchens, tightening those buttons, everything the sea sends away, writhing in senseless slack.

Build it to be on it or give away, the facial hesitancy of your progenitors showing up in every feel, letting doors down by not handling going through them, the window nothing more than square awareness, mashing land up in the linear result of the hand, cracked back into home or walking proposal, cast out—rusty environs of the body, to jug up in a pleasantry not unlike ice & vodka, building it to take where you came from one town over & drop it for voices, that it will ring there, keeping on w/direction, that steady pluck.

Tower in, flower out, into the cup & into the mouth, docking on a slant to stare back at what led us to be, pouch of flesh hooked from the line into the hand standing at the edges of land, worn to become another taking-out, notch of belt silence slept through, making ice recognize what it withholds, that we too grow young at the start of reason, asking the water to again be still until we cross it for the other fill, which is to move the shadows back to the light of their own shade, & to crest, as does the sent, into a glowing portion of the whole.

From the sea into the news, where we don't come around until the sharp blade spouts, & with the middle's pulse, dusk the welcome interruption lust lays into lull, cotton scarf around the upper body & air upon you, through the holes, taken as we are under tries & angles to be sure in the cull, between 3rd & 4th, gear or course, just as the noise cuts off where it told you it was doing something there, leaving you alone here.

As they will come to behind lens, prepped to coerce pasture between high tech lines, where authority is flattened gaze & our talked-about faces a place unplayed by the ends of day, that shoulder as it gyrates into lasso & breaks mares to surpass chance, guarded as we are in the silence of public violence, left to tinker with unconditional night, keeping gloved hands stilled behind stems, taking them off in the rows to pop a pull, to crop a feel.

They all see me leaning in—as I lean I am unraveled from torsoing crowd & I go quiet as allowed, to stop boarding larger worries by leaning more & more, the history on my unconcerned face a golden act of keeping the tides down, not returning sound's tongue, where inward the voice keeps saying, I will not stay, I will not go.

Be even quieter, stand here not knowing, splayed out as one is by pearls to divulge the throne, railing & remedy, lilted lip, aristocracy, washing your plate in front of the window, smashing it in your head, mimicking the sun by flipping your tongue into a ball & bowling the light out, how I try quietly for you, sieve of balcony & tragedy, always an accomplice of look, behind telling how we all run holes through eyes from the bottoming gums, then how you fill them up with diamonds, becoming more unknowable, shining against us all.

Again, this neighboring condition, plants & bottles for one another, a sound that comes in windows because the walls have been down on themselves, what the world would do if left alone as one farm, the fence determined to bring the country into sensible border, thatch & brick, ruffle, water & the slick latch that releases heat into the airy gate, clinking in salute, getting on to be one with it all.

He calls it solace, or soul's lace, or sentiment owned lightly as caring embraces, the wedding day on repeat, paled in strip malls as you retreat to permanent fall & bachelor laugh, spooking the dawdle, cresting the continent with a belt around disquietude, recycling night & super moon, as he blows smoke out the shape of himself, using the cigar as a candle before the night boogies out of surface, stiletto heel of longing, wool-knit strike of hand, where the petals hide before whisking into a whirl right out of land.

What you cannot stand for, standing alone for an exchange, basket that carries the plan back out to awning, as simple as that gets—moving toward another—before it hits that you're a lover in the large graph of wonder, staring back at your own face first thing in the morning, last thing in the night, believing that in between the views you own yourself & then to be alright, rolling the words away from your body each day, sucking them back through light.

Start them lined up to duck when the tunnel comes, to be proud or curious, to encourage lest our actions become injurious, this dog-found habit of the mouth staying open all day so that words are not invited in search, just the hitting our spots make when our feet leave grass, starting them out at karma—patient aggressors—then letting them run the sun down into shore, how it is to move & stand, to implore even more.

Everyone untying their shoes & glowing toward the water, unpiled as sun on the neck of the body, spine just a two-lane way to stay aligned with laps, needing movement before tomorrow & a day for freedom to raise its assigned colors into voice, blood in the sky, the night, balking back against itself & the freckling ankles & toes, only in summer where the full-time work can feel at rest, sucked on by sun, length of the body come flat for pounding cloud, bent quietly by sand.

Come back, sweet thing, now or as never is also something to grip, even if the slip follows & you are suddenly hands around a tree while the boat goes on, the day independence becomes dependent upon swaying midnight inebriates high on the break of war, hats on every table to remain there forever, including the one the decanter shattered before we sucked up the entirety of Bordeaux, wanting nothing but the scrap of phalanges, disparate eye control, blood in tannins & a vocalist streaming our vacancy across the sinking staccato of trust, as time becomes a silver circle on your wrist, waiting to catch the moon in reflect & to hush it w/fist, to let it all go.

Along the lines of all that you leave, that geographically speaking North America's toenail cuts into abrupt flowering discourse, where you are wiring memory so that you can return to what once couldn't fade & blow smoke through the kitchen as to put the lean against walls, our backs groped by wood, dead for having done nothing but have gleaned from where it stood, to shut up the mouth, to ask for nothing exterior from breathing as it begins somewhere within external sprint, integrand muscles cut for the united poise & plunge of our core, why that sort of trumpet humps upon the hush for the bass to break out of hibernation, to do a push-up where you have not been forgiven, to streak across cadence because of the other end, everyone naked carrying mirrors facing outward, asking questions about the oceans, like, how can we bouquet, &, if we must come to a border why must it be the most moving thing, even after we've come so far to get here?

They take you out in decades, breathing holes in high rises, slipshod drains, & you on your back keeping the whole frame glazed, as we are want to lighten for lines & squares but darken & disappear in all of the affairs, trafficking another loading of the long blue bar, gin & pixel, the sea like careless tin eroding at its base where we've never been ourselves, pinned to corral the shelves that the spines keep upright, the ages turned, as another roof bows to the heat, pressing the bodies down, closer, clicking them one by one right over.

I've been there but will keep it from you, early morning radio & skin crawl, 90 mph taxis on the River Parkway, running a horse out of fear near the docks, asking the sun not to show up so that you can get by w/o anyone pinching this truth, to stop allowing music to swallow your awakened mind, especially jazz cutting the pocket of sparrows into glints, the way time moves forward like a dry cough then how you request it peel something wet back, sickness in elation, memory, as if you can stack yourself there w/o your tics, a bypass unused until another is built & we drive around in squares offering our high rise homes to distant strangers, trains keeping on against rivers, needling the shiver, maining the lines.

That the mountain being there each morning is enough to keep you in a place, why we grow restless becoming ourselves in a space we cannot change, clouds entombed by factory plume, cars moving the world wider before tucking below & into the garage, mode of the chimes to touch your skin before you hear them rhyme into the up-&-coming sun, to be as we are undone to what we cannot remember, & if you want a road to where you feel comfortable alone, where the sky lines your history out on the horizon, shading the complete, the wheels keeping on as the feels repeat.

That you can & will take the head off the light, as much as we are flown away to unknowns while tucking in caution, awaiting the clean pinch of yes, the walls lined up like docked sails, winter slitting its existence in the snow, keeping inside the clothes while sleeping & the dream that stops at skin, coming back midday as the shadow we keep leaving between doors, thinking it won't disperse itself when the light widens, that even a speck of cool is enough to sentence us under, cover us up.

Down along the mall, window popping & stranger cropping, the real feel is the way of what is between us & the glass, shaking mannequins hands, kicking spiders, the overwhelming voice that rules the head when workers speak about retreating from social defeats, that the voice keeps saying, why this, &, stop talking to me, I won't be here for long, but then how you will be, & how the world will see you as sanction for solitude, image too, bruised into playback, what you refer to in liking someone's hair even if you walk away not knowing what color it is, groping potions with indifference, the national public radio in your boots, trying on a suit before taking it off in the wish fountain & crying your fucking parts out.

In the middle of it again, not stuck but there, in the middle bordering doubt & what makes a bird go out of tune a word grow out of ruin, the speech that retrieves the globe-hollow theories we relieved ourselves of, hurrying out of ethics, full water glass with ice to thaw back in, that you drink it right as the last cube descends itself, this liquid-only riot where land too stands to fail, leaving you out in the undocked sash of wind & the top floor wave that rides in behind you, flushing you out of find.

I have not told you yet but I've been putting on a suit & sleeping in every park around, waking up to feel my cigarettes smashed & piecing them back into freckled suck, holding them through flame & into my body's frame, believing in the breathing I'm proceeding without, as the arms lose themselves in dreams & we're never meant to be hanging out with them all day, shaking their digits, palming the chests & napes & asses & mistaking the top of our heads for a closed dome, polishing old woes where the mouth rewinds.

Border of the other, on steps representing precaution, tie hung on the cigar's tip, that we are celibate when sympathizing, relating the third story down on page two, getting halfway through a tomato before realizing it is green, everything between process & passion & that you cannot speak the latter or inculcate the former, saying everything directly to the mirror—dear reflection, forget me here—before breaking the windows down to the sand they expanded from before demand, before shore, tapping each granule out from horror.

She wants nothing to do with it & she's been seen in a solo elsewhere, unflagging & archival, cinched by the fullness of survival, all the kin of war torn into capitals & color tones, what your teeth do with no one around uttering the word liberty in a forest, shouldered to hold the past so high it can't see the present stuttering at its anklet, the rose diamond of memory & if what happened there seams here, cloaked flower hat & the realization that our eyes worsen over time simply because we've seen enough, or that there's been nothing yet to see.

In the crowd you cannot hear it but you are watching it, then holding transfer to your head, if what can be heard will reappear in the thread of your nearest step out of sound & light, poking into dots & relieving, tenderly, the rendering of these eaves, art as it parts way w/itself in frames, to feel close to the system that confounds you then to leave yourself in it as you wander around it, judgement & rage, speech cutting into stats the spit plugs into slats the tongue tucks back, to swallow that appeal, jacketed in the moon, waiting for all the tiny things to stop happening, including you, voiceless in the hoist.

It is still there on the corner, strung up to enlighten dust, cinema as we knew it best to tighten behind ticket & box, wringing the unreal, to look alike one another until voice lunges us into the whole precision, all the animal words dying in rivers, carried into white caps the sea flaps back, & how frenzied we become when belief surpasses knowledge, to be certain of something purely from how the blood turns the brain on, the bravest coordinate of becoming something more than ourselves, as the wind will relieve a leaf from being hung.

Serious about the brawl, crowds always measuring up to something taller, louder, the lead in the dog w/o leash, America steadies its sunglasses, hairnet, paragon of the face, polka-dots of the breast & deciding what's best when the lens arrives to run you out of your cowboy time, dreams so consistently sexual you cannot finish a sentence with a stranger w/o kissing them out of continuum, never hearing what confession comes out of their lips, resistant in the flip, or yours, insistent on tipping it all over.

Shape as we undo it in moving the contour, breath tipping the tongue into sentence, proving for everyone something is inside this little token hutch of hold, this forgotten flower, that we flee over direction in order to feel at home in sitting still, as the light rides our skin until the bones darken back to traditions, as seeing is just where the eyes go when the mind overflows, & speaking what the mouth does when the mind tries not to blow out, to the eyes through the river blood a rise in floods of touch, that we'll be keeping on the coast but never living it, never picking the rock up to see the wet imprint return to a flat grain of life in time that still remains, pain beneath each stance slain.

When the horses are gone we hit the field & straighten our stances in the wait, holding corn stalks up to our mouths to whistle back the truth from gallop, that the full moon fucked us over & ran the mares off the cliff, that the television is the end of you doing anything for yourself, anything at all, portioning out images with square care, unaware of what recedes in the stare, fixated on slitting the knobs & cornering the numbers, your dumb throb, your numb sink, the mares rubbed away in the wind's blink.

The rein returns with neigh but no bodies, as residential as we can become in a national park, wrung out of city, fast through the path in the aftermath of parked cars & the voting we do for the world, checking off the box, always a box, the alarm that is a cricket in the racket of the week's thicket, that you hated coming to work every minute because when the day ended you were no longer in it.

Both here, one with the shirt out, the other with the hint in the smirk, theatrical in the splash, waiting for the field to filter through the fence & shut the cultures flat, the tone of zooming outward with awaiting, for the hot nothing summer slums from, sweating through the cubes, the south inside its northern self, flannels that end at the toes, the frame hands work while getting cut up & dirtied, attending all the rows of silence, as good as a boat can be in the middle of a highway, a boy sitting with the sail across states, the motor with no idea where to spin, lines between the lines within.

And another America leaving as you hold your histories out on a pole, crossing the line that hangs outside the whole, a parade working through sense unused, flecked to jangle in the far-angled manner of the moon, locality inside the guitar, bunched-up wonder & the worlds that happen inside us while waiting for change, fixed as we are to run the dreams off & say we don't know why they went that way, why faces climbed into stride with red & white & blue & fled until the night fucked them through.

You can't splay it that way, the first recording happening on an island, letting everyone here know that if they enter where you've just left they better pry open their fortunate lights, as we all remember seeing inside ourselves & leaving beside ourselves, the wound not-listening becomes, & the argument between yourself & altruism that carries on each step you make in public, as relation is in relation always to the self & an other, as it's no longer tether where we push to where the answers pull, where we weather on in unscripted lull, pleasuring ourselves where we cannot be culled.

Last age in the look & you don't want to get there, racism always slow dancing in an empty kitchen between knife & window, lives taken out of themselves by mission & morale, the death of spontaneity, that you'd feel better being placed in unfamiliar vans & driven to national parks with strangers if you knew you wouldn't have to return to a building, how the hot springs keep spitting out the unworked agendas of time, your legs during the run a passage, undertone, riveted by outlines & then how up in the face we'll get defending our rights, fists in pockets until sanity ignites.

FOUR

AN solo bush of ... into a loop, ... with condoms hands, ... this way ... fans, how the stars same in abandoned ... lup, the real idea ... when you tied your

... I return to you at ... long ago, peeling out of ... outsides, and I know that ... I see is along in their ... when I speak directly ... contain that we keep our ... do more bells, but ... drop out of rhythm, and ... you and I are wiping up ... come along in an agreement, ... put in this country ... to your painted apparel, ... others with rhizomes at old ... side-winding ... again and ... that I return to this place

... background is the abyss ... underwater, stacks of 1000s ... spaced to creep forward into ... as your fingers are gone ... in the tank, ... the country chatter ... out in a line, that ... a handling, ... the brass trio of hands and ... access takes you ... into silk skits of dying ... the primary mug for ... there, the canvas belt ... per all the leaving ... sitting out and in front

... and you don't ... always ... lives taken ... and more ... that you ... in unfamiliar ... in ... how the ... the universe ... less during ... pulsing ... up in the ... our phone, ... insanity ignites.

LESS OR MORE THAN THIS MAINSTREAM, LEDS AS PLOWED TO AWKEN VORTICAL, HORIZONTALLY THE LIGHT RIBS IN A PINK BRONCO TO SMARTLY DISCUSS ENGINE OF US ALL, THE CULL IN HOARY AIR, THAT A PURGE IS ... FICTION WAS BEFORE THIS BUT, ... WE GROW UP A NEW HERD AND ... IT CROSSOVER, THAT WORDS DO ... AMBITION AND YOU MUST WATCH ... SUNG OUT TO TOUCH THE ... IN, CLOSING DOWN WITH ... A SPECIFIC TIME WHERE ... GOINGS WHAT YOU CANNOT.

... DESK, MAKING FAMILY ... AT THAT A WAGON PULLED ..., ELEPHANT SPRAWLED ..., PORTIONING THE ... UMBRELLA FOR THE SUN ... WORLD HURLED INSIDE ... SHALL WE CHOOSE TO ... THE ENGINE, WHAT ... PROTECT WHEN THE ... INTO THE GARDEN, ... SWOOPING ACROSS TRUNKS ... RUNNING THIS BLOOD AND ... TO SAY THAT IS AMERICA ... FEELING NEITHER SMALL ... IN ITS RUGGED CAUSE.

... RECEIVING WHAT LIGHT RELEASES ... OF THE WOODS, THAT A FOREST IS WORTH THIS CHORUS, TO RECEIVE PAY OR PAIN, A CANTELOPE SO SUN ORANGE YOU LET IT ROLL OUT ON ITS OWN, OFF THE TABLE, DOWN THE STAIRS ... OUT THE DOOR AND INTO THE GRASS, WHAT EUROPE DID SECRETLY TO SUPPRESS THIS LIVING STATESIDE PURPLED BY RENT AND LEANING HILLTOPS BENT AGAINST THE SOFT FINGER, TO GO UNDER WITH IT WHEN THE ISLAND REMEMBERS IT STARTED OUT BELOW.

IT'S THE SAME YEAR BUT THE TIME IS RUNNING LOOSE, STAYING INLAND THE WEATHER OF SOMETHING NOW JUST REVERBERATING RETREAT, HOW WE WERE TAUGHT WITH RULERS TO LAKE AROUND OUR HANDS AND PICK UP PAINT WITH PLASTER, WITH PLASTER AND THE DISASTER WHICH IS BECOMING SOMETHING WE RECKON, AS YOU CAN WIDEN BEFORE TURN AND REGIST GLANCE, THE OTHER ARTS YOU HAVEN'T TRIED OUT JUST AS MUCH A PART OF THE OVERALL DOUBT YOU MUST PROTECT, LEAVING THE CITY TO KEEP TO OTHERS SILENCE, THE PATTERN OF MEETING THAT SCRUBS THE DOOR AND KEEPS THE FIELD STITCHING ITS WIND FOR MORE RAIN, TO REDDEN THAT GARDEN AND RUN THE SEA WITHIN IT, TO FATTEN THEM.

HANDLING THE ROPES, STEEL AND STRAW COMMANDING MORE DEPENDENCE FROM THE SHIFT, ALWAYS NEVER MEANING THAT IN ALL WAYS WE ARE AFFORDED TOMORROW IN TURNING AROUND TODAY WITH FIREWORKS, SOMETHING UP THERE YOU HAVE NOT MET REGRETTING WHAT THEY LIKE YOU TO DO, PRODUCTION, EXCLUSION SUN STICKING THE FAN WITH ITS GARAGE HOVERING ALL THE WAY OUT FROM WHAT HAPPENS BETWEEN COASTS, THAT CONCUR LOCKS NO DIFFUSION MANY BREAKS LATER SHOWING UP AS SLEEPING, IGNORED AS WE ARE TO STAND IN WEATHER AND SEND SOMETHING SLOW, HAMMER IN HAND.

4/10/13

SLIP OR THE ARCH HANGING THROUGH THE CORRIDORS AND THE EMPTY VOLUMES RUSH OF THIS CAR'S BACK AT A SCARRED WIND WANTING TO CONTINUE REFERENCING NOT BECAUSE WE'VE NEVER BEEN INVITED TO WHERE IT DOESN'T MATTER, THE OTHER SIDE WITH FLOWER POTS CRAFTED INTO STUDIO TO TURN THAT DESTRUCTION AROUND AND FIND OUT WHAT YOU DO WHICH THROWN ALL FOR MONTHS, CROSS-REFERENCING RUBBISH AND THE RAW AREA, ATTEMPTING TO FLOAT THEM INTO THE SAME LANGUAGE WITHOUT WATER, BREAKING OUT OF THE DESK TO FISH OUT TOWARD THE ROCK, RUNNING A TOE IN THE CRACK AND THEN THE SPLASH

3/10/13

PRODUCING THE GREAT LEAP FORWARD, THE PATTERN DISORDER AROUND THE TURN, GOING TO BE STRAIGHT AHEAD, PLOT OF THAT IN THE INDUSTRY'S OVERSTRETCHED ..., RISING NEAR THE ENDS OF DEMAND, AT HOME HOW SIGNIFICANT THE DINING BAR AND OUR FINGERS PINCHING SALT, AN ARTICULATED GENE SPOOLING THIS MENTAL OF PROCESS, SPECKLED POSTING AND NEXT WATCH ON THE RUN A SENIOR FOR SLIPPING CAPACITY'S VISIT BACK INTO ROW, THE HIGH RISE RIDE IN FLUX AT THE PARK OF THE NIGHT, HOW WE KEEP COMPANY WITH MITIGATED AIM IN OUR ...

... with another in this line of your language, postures of clouds on the ground, the strange sound of planes getting their garden posture on, as rugged as others will allow us to be before settling into compliances, making a mixing, any more for the first time and how can cannot recall the exact words of anyone dead or alive in a row, just that they sometimes started and added places to grow

7/10/13

AS IF TO RETREAT, poking a toe through slant, shooting out around the side of ... in full sprint toward it ... I follow the leaving of ... in the air it leaves a ... those deep cornfields ... stop from cars, far ... runs from the past to ... streak I flew through ... newfound, how tracks ... with sunflower skin and

over in the small signs ... lean, every knot clustered ... the smaller grid for which ... from the plane's window of ... cavities, to run all new ... we have to trace for, but ... we are by transit, turning ... strong and water, destroyed ... when the town opens its ... the sounds crash out across ... found being what they are ... through streets, leaving the ... running slower up and down ... your slippers

THE SHADOW REMAINS itself into reflection, proof that your body would not let ... crowded in this bone, the ... comes back up a bent place ... sun to scene, trading the ... the water and slow gun, ... picture and blurry stop line ... who were coming in this and ... something antique, but our ... the intrigue simplicity blown ... into, letting it be the sizes ... of analogies and how I fear ... by dinner table swans, or the ... picture comes down and the window

SLIP IT IN, GET THE ... BRING IT BACK BEFORE ... THIS ONE WHICH KNOW ... THE EVERYDAY WITH THEY ... AN EVERYDAY, LIFTING ... INTO THE LAMP AND SPINNING ... ON ITS FOOT, BUNDLED ... BEING POINT, THE ... HOOD IN THIS POINT ... THE ... INTERLUDE WHICH ... TO THE CORNER THE LINE ... AND ESCAPING FROM THE GUN ... GONE A SMALL LEAVING SEA ... GONE AS WELL SO THAT YOU

RESPONSIBILITY AS IT TAKES YOU INWARD, ESCALATION OF THIS IMAGE STORING UP FOR EXITS AND RETRIEVALS FLIPPING THE OTHER SIDE TO WHERE IN QUESTION YOU AGAINST MEAN TO HIDE WHAT CAN HAPPEN ALONG FOR YOU IF THE ANSWER IS YES, RAIN THAT CUTS HIGH AND JAMS IT BACK FOR US TO BREATHE BACK IN THE WATER BLUE AND LAMELLA DESERT SCUTTLE, HOW I GROW MY IVANS NOT LEAN BUT LONG AND NOT THE GUITAR BUT FOR WHAT I CAN DO IN CONTINUING TO CUT ALL, THAT I CAN CARRY THAT EXTRA BREATH EVERYWHERE AND RETURN TO YOU AS THE DOOR OPENS, FULL OF RAINBOW FLOWERS

... FIRST THING YOU DO IS SLAM, ... HEAR IT OVER THOSE GOING ... ON AIR, FOR THE COLD BOMB BURST ... OF REVOLUTION RESIDENCE IN THIS ... AS TO UNLOCK EMOTION WE ... OUR TEETH ALL NIGHT THINKING WE'D ... PLAY OUT IN DEPTHS ENGAGE AND ... ACCEPT AS CARVED, AS HOW IT IS ... DRAWING GARY BREAKS OVER ONE ... YOU AND CARRY EVERYTHING YOU THE ... THE MARKET OUT IN YOUR HAND, ... POTATO FOOT FOLD THE VODKA, THE ... THAT POURED TOO QUICK TO STICK

...reads the animals into the night, your marks it out... in dirt...cut we like silk... power of wind... are, where we wrap... need to expand... culture persona... bad, that the... full picture from... at the overpass... belong us to border...

...ose again youth, instrument you meet... up only to let it... mud the real thing... cards around work... not controlled by... as outside your own... this day corroding... just that, to... you in as a drug... ribs you out, the... inside of legs... outside itself an art... the soul so... it's just a mining...

Neighborly watch, this time thing you do to not be alone in a country, bringing your dog out in a canoe to the island, kneeling on those with what burns, don't do what words won't crow for the now out into land, that we keep working in records factory has always been there, strokes of architecture not put, as we are asked to reconfigure ourselves our sketchings, leaving water, line our toes as under our feet this water plans to enclose more land...

They will tell you the painter must always begin with line, even if it sees itself when the colors beg to care for one another, as our strokes the long sight of them lines into moving flesh and that phone was... for accurate color thus oil, never found it in the middle of painting the portrait he didn't just reveal and paint himself as she feels him, or run a brush across that low...

...out, as youth will always... a jewel, plywood to... is only as hard as its... stars you because it came... the look is unhappy... life is too, for all is as... you waste it to wonder...

We stuff the flowers that give... of not swimming in our own... feel that row, that row... already with thoughts and... what's up below the exit...

At this high lean singing through the break, recalling something that has not happened in front of all the open doors, sleeping alongside the mirror with ten set alarms, keeping on about how the rectangular table should be carved into an oval because we all think too fucked up...

There has never been anything more compelling than a long smooth leg planting from your position the long landing drop of breath, a leg on the... of a city or cloth never caught to hold the leg in and keep it there because it must be moving out to... and taking air, destination...

...it there curled up with words tucked under, any exertion... to arrive somewhere... where you ache, giving your... over to breasts...

The glass window trusts the shopper no less or more than the mannequin, our legs as plighted to align vertically as horizontally the light rides in on a pink bronco to smash & distress the engines of us all, the curl in our heavy air, that a curse is what friction was before dust, lest we open up new hides & coat the mind overnight with choice, that words do leave your head & you must walk the clotheslines out to touch their threads back from the dead, closing down the sign to be a specific time inside yourself, where stillness becomes what you cannot.

This, the other task, making family happen, a wagon pulled over roadside, everyone sprawled out in cylinders, portioning an offspring, umbrella for the sun & the lost world hurled back inside our stride, that we choose to start again the engines of the past, what petal you'd protect when the town charges into the garden, flashlights sweeping across trunks & legs, running the blood & root loose, to say this is America w/o pause, feeling neither small nor grand in the rugged cause.

Above, how the roads are lines, the acres staked-out squares, & how we speak nothing of this on land, thinking we're turning this four-wheeled motor red against the blue, green, & grey, out for a breathing stint with the blanket memory has troubled over stones, a basket of food & our backs against the mountains, which stand like old-school cardiograms up to the sky, asking nothing of how the church pierces the middle of the farm, draining angel blood into organ & bell, & the sound of crowded trees displeasing we who've held secrets in the backs of our eyes, untucking our shirts at the end of the drive, the worn-out silvering lights burned out of our veins, swept back into the belt.

Lining up for the appreciation brigade, trains receiving what light
relieves itself of in the woods, that a forest is worth this chorus, to
receive pay or pain, a cantaloupe so sunset orange you let it roll on out,
on its own, off the table, down the stairs, out the door & into the grass
where the sun smashes it into the mash-up, what Europe did secretly
to surpass living in stately asides, perplexed by rent & leaning high-
rises bent against the Hudson to repent, to go under with the island to
where it started long ago.

Responsibility, as it takes you inward, escalation of the inhalation, storing up for exits & retrievals, flipping the other side to where in a question you really mean to hide what can happen alone for you if the answer is yes, rain that cups heat & jambs it back for us to breathe, in the water bulge & lamping desert scuttle, how I grow my nails not lean but long & not for guitar but for what I can do in continuing to cut air, that I will carry that extra breath everywhere & return to you as the door opens, full of rounded flowers.

Handling the pipes, steel & show, commanding more dependence from the shift, never meaning we are affordable in having risen today with fireworks, duds, something up there you have not met repeating what it would like you to do—production, exclusion, sun sticking the fan with its gripe—hollering all the way out from what happens between coasts or coats, the newfound lyrical coterie, that concern looks no different many decades later showing up as discipline, ignited as we are to stand in weather & sing something slow with hammers in our hands.

As if to retreat, poked, or in toe-tipped slant in our plantings arrive revoked, memory's around the side of the house in full sprint toward the park, & I follow the leave of her dress in the air as it lessens & pause, the deep cornfield effect & the steep draws from a better thaw into sectors of the seed, farming in golden rows, from foot past head the endless stalks I flow through after my newlywed, her tracks rusted with sunflower skin & sunshine thinned to gloss into invisible future, that real glow into the hoed-down dirt, graphing among stone, that we'll keep on together, running right out of alone.

Slip or the arch hanging through the corridors & the choppy voluminous push of the cab's back at scabbed wind, wanting to continue referencing nature because we've never been invited to where it doesn't matter, the other side with flower pots crashed into shadows, to turn that destruction around & find out what you do when taken alone for months, cross-referencing Brooklyn & the Bay area, attempting to flatten them into the same language w/o water, breaking from the deck to feel out toward the dock, running a toe in the crack & splash, widening life to last.

For centuries, just an invitation to dance & now the solo rush of moving from self into a purpose loop, keeping the room held up with the conductor's hands, the presidents on the walls replaced with flashes of your name, how the stars start their own game in abandoned lakes before splintering waves into tips, into sea-scattered lip, the real idea scuttling the spine when you hold your hands on your hips in observing the community dancing line, that as any urge grows warmer the mind must grow calmer, clothes slipped off to run the entire spread w/o anything but animal eyes, to view the green unraveling from your feet, the rough nudge, your flag for trudging up love.

Time for another respite, what dots accept one another in the line of your language, posters of clouds on the ground, patches of grass in the sun, the endless sound of planes getting their early altitude on, as resilient as others will allow us to be before settling into complacency, making mood by move, any move for the first time, & how you cannot recall the exact words from anyone dead or alive in a row, just that their sentences started & parted there to grow.

It's the same year but the tide is running loose, shaking inland, of everything now just reverberating retreat, how we were taught with rivers to lake against our hands & fuck up—first with plaster, then with flirtation & disaster—which is becoming the thing that follows, as you can widen before tuck & resist glare, the other arts you haven't tried out just as much a part of the overall doubt you must protect, leaving the city to kelp at other tranquilities, the pattern of meshing that screens the thought & keeps the field stitching its wind away from the door for more rain, then to reopen the garden & run the sea within the scene.

The pride is readymade, born in the bone, where we wave entire homes above us & recite the rhyming roam about going heavy into the night, piano music that never makes it out of its shell, spinning in the residue, elbowed into the wall, that we love silk falling over us as result of wind, cutting into coverage, jutting from verge where we wrap up the lengthening need to expand, to march with the cultural persona back into truck beds or vintage swig, that the driver will hit it full throttle then release the clutch at the overpass, breaking through the fence, asking us to buckle up into the immense.

Consider again youth, what instrument you first picked up only to let it down, mud, the real thing you'd carry around were you not controlled by sounds outside your own, to leave this city certain it wants just that, to take you in as a drug & ride you out, the art inside of life taking life outside itself into art, controlling the solo mug so that it is no longer just a miming marimba bumped against air, then to spin your ditty there.

Yes me, no you, or yes to them who know the road cranks into a small neighborly laugh, the tiniest thing to be alone in a country— bringing your dog out in a canoe to the island, keeping on there with what birds don't do, with what words won't croon anew, then thumbing back the land, that we keep walking in it because property has always been theft, these stories of architecture, not plot, as we are robed to incomplete ourselves on shorelines, letting water line our toes as under our feet the water flows to enclose more land, the tree tilting down from above to tease the instance out of matter.

Over in the song quiet frequencies lean into unrepeatable beat, every notch clustered as to be a lighter grid for what we see from the plane's window, passing dying counties, to run news in on a horse, sign it, travel for it via pamphlet, bulldozed as we are by transit, turning against stone & water when the town opens its week & the sounds creak out before being found doing what they do, to feel up fate through the sheets, etching dreams by running slowly up & down our sleeping reams of hair.

As the first thing you do is silent, lest they hear it over there going down on air, revolution reddened in the weave, as to unsleeve emotion we grind our teeth in the night, thinking words will flatten out in dusted enamel & our ancestry will starve, how it is to arrange empty baskets over one another, to resign & carry everything we own for the market in our hands—the potato that failed the vodka, the tomato that paled too quick, that you keep arriving everywhere a shadow of what cannot stick.

It's the only glowing thing in the room & you don't touch it—you pull your hat above your ears & clutch your hands so they don't expand into light that isn't your own, in the stabbed ticket receipt of existing, in the grander piano no walls will shroud, winter sitting only for a shelf portrait here, wanting to reveal the compartment inside of the larger satchel of logistics, as you go on not touching it, depth & meaning, feeling every grace graze you in the aisle while you linger in produce, new shipments in the bells & boats, promise as something no one takes outside themselves anymore.

Slip in, get the days off & bring the past back before the freeze, this one touch wonder where you know how to control the everyday w/o effort, lifting another decade into the lamp & springing the reed upon its root, bundled to receive the bone point, the piano the party dunked in the pond before wearing the seedy globe of community back to the den, to hold a clarinet over everyone & declare sound a one-holed golden sitter, a god, the crosses atop the chapels bruising the sky back into systematic hue, unworn wind.

When the shadow remains, pressing itself into reflection, presenting what your body would not let itself be alone, crouched in the bone, the building comes back up a better place for the sun to scene, tracing the skin with ice water & sloe gin, putting family pictures over every shop window to see who will come inside & not expect something of themselves, coins of intrigue simplicity blends trouble into, letting it be the unseen arrival of anxieties & heartbreak varnished by dinner table silence, or that the picture comes down as the window continues.

And here the interlude, people you know of but have never met slitting the silhouette, cars passing through their heads, their legs lost in sidewalk cracks then the sideway shades of midtown heart attacks, flapping their mouths into the private microphone, voice flanking your surroundings into false rain, a simile never more than an excuse to get past how real it was when you couldn't find match for what isn't yours, language, turning in your broadening gait to perspire throughout the entire holiday, raising the family flag in your hand, that windy independence, before pulling it apart & floating in the speaks.

They will tell you a painter must always begin with line, even if it loses itself when the colors settle for one another outside the defined, as our shins pipe the long heat of their vines into moving flesh & that there is need for its accurate color, thus oil, never knowing if in the middle of painting her portrait we didn't just reverse it & paint ourselves as she feels us, or run a brush across her low neck to take sense into the curve, where the wall keeps doing things, like adorning itself in thin blankets, streaking in the thin stamp of facts, with other horses ailing in the backdrop, that it's okay to starve there with belief.

Cleared out, as youth will unravel a jewel in the reminisce, flowered to prepare history as only as hard as its seams, stabbing you because it cannot tackle, the look unready because the life is too, for anyone is as you wish them to wonder, songs coming out of neighborhood windows w/o genre, placing your hands on their reach, what has come along before forcing us forward for more, & to be prepared, to flick an ant out of its crack & let the oil of your skin in, to where the spreading cut toward a belonging begins, the stem of an untouched stretch.

Oh & for everything to lie like that, aware that we end line & structure each time we bend with the mend of clothing, every tincture a puncture & how the wrists fall listlessly over our own torsos, smacked into that short-lived fullness, to have at direction & spill over the bed, to then be led into flush touch, that slow make of us, that first take at courting something central before spinning outside ourselves, where the real inside sits, split from its hide.

From reflection this is our mistake, not knowing who it is that passes for us in mirrors & here where a shadow slants across the drape, of sun a foolish disguise for straightforwardness, each angle a hint that we are slits in the whole sprinting glint, slotted & wheeled on the four-lane freeway, to be a way that is free, a ledge come out of belted hinge, a tough thigh dabbed with jeans & cotton, & to beat the game with a rivulet of breath behind the monologue stretch, words which come out of the block of mouth in quick herds of intent, context what makes the heat & the light sneak the shade, drawing your outline on a window into fade, delivering the mode.

Sure enough, I've been in a river making sense of stuff, most specifically how urge can become a thing, as it starts singing off-key to discreetly play the whole street or night straight, as much as we make our hair unaware of the scalp's clouding roam, & in this swirl the girl who comes to the door to leave fate in a simple twist w/o waiting, growing back into the field the land won't resist—everything as it at once is one—or when the union sails you through idiot winds, into shapes the room grooms for replay, blasting you here, into the tides, to where you churn on full display.

Found it there curled up with the words tucked under, any direction an expectation to arrive somewhere other than where you are, ceding your realities to dreams, following astrology off the tongue of the believers into matter, leaving ballads where the head bends the pillow into catch, as much as we forgive shadows for spreading out & thinning when we cannot trace the space they've made in pinning us in the unrepresented, the crackle & cinch of unplanted clarinets on a windowsill, pushing them off the ledge, running down to catch them before they wail out at the end.

Your envy of the tree up there & that it won't leave, that its reach does not return to refresh or sully up the head, scrubbing bricks on bark, the one chirp forgotten in the middle of the release, that rooftops are the real graves the sky can do something painless with, sight carried into you for longer than you can learn your way through it, where you want to move toward while attending the end of the novelty, a ledge, fruit, flipping back some other wind that will reassemble & thimble the whole, or outside it where the tree slits a pot to flower the line of your reach.

A long smooth leg unspooling from periphery, lush landing in plush drag of breath, a leg on the chaise or between 6th & 5th, pattern of a city or cloth never enough to hold the limb in & keep it because it must be moving out to click & tangle air, destination never more rare than when the leg culls itself smooth there, heels or flats not even to compete with that hot flashing branch of body, gliding into a midnight circle, to step the Charleston out of its past & shake its length, its beauty, vast.

We stuff the flowers that give signs of not surviving into our hats & align for that row, that pew, the year billed already with holidays & funerals, knowing what's up below the suit or dress & that a face can tell you nothing sometimes, perhaps that it is only the deliverer of what gets prattled & hinged inside, a cheers that rattles & chimes in earrings & how the bones ruin time behind the flesh, as beauty will always stop these wonders & spelunk them into dimensions beyond blunder, the tension between wanting to touch & knowing that it would end you, that your hands would brush out the petals on way to untying the braids, that if the neck showed up you'd snap.

Dear Light, as in repose, you are a flower somewhere here, near middle, the middle, tusks that pile you out, parting for where the button carries on w/o thread, genesis of body's herbed & inward shelf, why it makes sense to take yourself out drink by drink to drunk, your glass skeleton & the valve-cubes creeping the liquid, chipping the flow, to ask at last for all the dank chances you can come home with to pulse, & how you'll hold them into one shape, awaking as one always does to the thought that here is there.

She sits down to draw herself but it isn't happening, it isn't a pearl or neck, the mirror refusing to reflect what was put in there—downcast eyes failing even to forward the notion of self, that we grow out of water still parched & solo in the tended garden, your lasting effect always that it's quieter to be in the shade when you cannot perfect the feelings or the age, or to resurrect through the hand's impulse a fade in the cranked-out ray, pardoned to restrict, a toughened spin for the fingers that do nothing now but shake, leaning back against your chair to find that your back isn't even there.

Can't figure it, can't stick the now, keep a top hat in hopes of having one memory from tonight hold itself in, can't even find the other centuries within the ribs, wrapping a palm over cane, nudging photographs of things younger than your drive into the night, wondering what's come over you like lamp shade, like wet sweater, like opening a door to the street that keeps saying it will bring you into the middle of the orchestra & drown you there, inside the piano, inside intermission, drilled into your condition.

At this high lean singing through the break, recalling something that has not happened in front of all the opened books, sleeping alongside the mirror with ten set alarms, keeping on about how the rectangular table should be carved into an oval because we wring the night too fucked up, hung in quadrants with the corners flown inside us, dusting off the family matter by counting breath, stepping on ants, whispering the word America in elevators with our hats on.

She's thinking & the world stops again, as easy as it is to strap the self senseless in the light & turn the street off, every walk an aside for the river we'll be wading in, mist that sucks against itself to shroud the outside, keeping on with seed, the angles in a hot bob of need, scarves that do everything to the neck a hand cannot, as you have a unwinding stamp in that sight & it juts its jitter mid-air, grooved & sending, a glove along the city line & the streets retreating into themselves beat by beat, all breath paused as you remain, sinking in your untapped feet.

I confess now that I've climbed too far into this mess of images not my own, that I knew existentialism briefly but then my hair grew out & I couldn't get through with you but yes, yes the world is itself while inhaling & near nothing in the release of breath, so loaded on our necks these bobbling heads, the suede & a collar that bulks & dips, expecting the mouth to river words inside of it, freaked out by dust, fog that keeps showing up trying to remind us of density & intrusion, the propensity we have for disclosing problems in an attempt at inclusion, yet here we are, over a moving pen, the other side a fire w/o end.

And patrons overseeing this, the hosts of this show, spray a deep nothing from their collected hands, a spine of buttons running down the front of stance, that they won't be popping open or drawing closed but in diligent rows keeping the theme spun back into untouchable harmony, in how we act w/o our hands trying to make point, marching like sand, delivering an expression that ends living rooms, all day that night-ending sentence making its way from the brow to the lip, in wrinkle & ruin, to the mouth that replicates the moon.

As all background is the above ground come underwater, stacks of ideas unprepared to steep forever in the body, releasing as your friends are done brining the hair, pulled back into the Sunday chair to heave the world out in respite, that we knew we'd be a handle, unturned in the long brass trip of hands & how one passage takes you alarmingly outward, into silk slots of dying hydrangeas, the thinking here for all that there, the candles bent to carry on for the leaving we've mismanaged, melting around the stems.

I return to you as I first came long ago, feeling out of myself & undertow, & I know that every person I see is alone in their relativity, that when I speak directly it is to resurrect outside of deflection—the shared contention that we keep our cells as churches do their bells—but let me stop, step out of rhythm, & admit that you & I are wrong if what has come along in life is not an agreement, that I throw a fit in this century as I'm stuck to time's pointed arrivals, to open up to others with theories as old as this tradition's archival pose, side-winding slim boy with a tough face & the ideas that grew into this space, I groom them until I return to myself & take place.

As you now know, as it could not be otherwise, as a pulse groans below the V-neck sweater, as a person happens between lamps & frames, fucking gods out of the room by staring, & how we are all cut by glass everywhere in between, this glittering hesitation is just lust stuffed up inside itself, in your sleep, as you knew then how to follow a heart out of a party & feel it up with a cigarette, as numb as we can get hitting it & hitting it, as it can only be otherwise, each decade misplacing us so that we long not for them but what they kept out, pointing at the future with a gun.

The crack in the room is where the pictures spill out, the room becoming noise moving into the solo observatory of sleep, where we're crossing the park to meet everyone from the past in a night-long journey toward outlasting our feed, as if resting is just meant to reproach then call out the truth of what has passed, so that we can stand up, sort the pictures on the table, & walk out of squares, into the air of timeless gales, out of our questionnaires.

You hold the bird in your hand each day at noon, to arrest flight &
favor, flesh over feather, throb over air, & then to paint with what is
left over or under there, where light takes the lines of a cage on its
way to shadow, as restless as we are cornering ideas as we awaken
to find our legs ready to release them, held close to replicate & not
abandon proximity, planes that consistently get lost in their own
flow, the passionate peripatetic, wanting sound to stop consisting of
surrounding, & puddle instead in one uninterrupted line to the shore,
as you don the night by keeping inside the head for more search, then
go through feather & bone into the private unreachable church.

All stacks into face, refining terms to rest on the flesh, holding body after its simulacrum, all the tugs of a boat from these elbows, the beggar's bush, betting on the sort of glint in your eye that relieves you of place, the kill, to move to you w/o letting you out of your skin, doing the room behind you with your mood, wearing a suit to stamp religion flat against its bloodless back & then canning the loss, shelves that cram you in your home during the roam, that you are there, far away, always defeating air.

The interlude is exuding the cloth, nude & in every lean a small leaving yet a coming-into as well, so that you are core or cause in the fenced reflection, we with our local imaginations not knowing what to do when the sky gets by w/o including you, light, all the pastel that remains in black & white—our produce of the head—studying the hands for hours forgetting they've been so outrageously there & everywhere neglectfully here, touching brush & brushing touch, how remaining we are in taking name & locking on.

FIVE

THE FREQUENCY BEFORE IT W...
COVERED, PUTTING YOUR FINGERS IN...
FRAME AROUND YOUR FACE TO...
...HOW YOU ARE NO LESS A P...
...PRIZE THAN THE WALL'S EYES, GUE...
...DARKNESS FORGOTS TO MAKE YOU A...
ABOVE WHEN YOU LOSING THE STA...
...FURTHER AFFAIRS, LIKE HOLDING...
...DOOR OPEN JUST FOR THE WIND...
...IT WILL BRING THE GOD OR...
...IN TO DROWN YOU WHERE...
...FIRST BUILT A HOME, A...
...IS ONLY MADE FOR EACH...
OF US WHEN WE CAN OWN IT...

...WILDLANDS AND IRON BOW...
THE PLEATS OF WIRE CLADDING LEAVES
DESTROYING OVER THIS POND OR IF THE
STARTED OUT ALONG WHEN THE FOURTH
PERIOD ITSELF BEGINS + AROUND HIM,
OR THAT IT'S YOU LOOKING TOO HARD AT
SOMETHING THAT ISN'T HERE YET AND
EVEN IF IT WILL BE THAT IT IS NO MORE
VISIBLE THAN YOUR TIDCOAT, CARRYING A
TRACING FROM A CUP'S LAST
HAND, YOUR FEELING, THAN
EVERYTHING UNBEGUN WHEN
YOU BEGIN THE DAY, SINCE
THE LAST DESPAIR A FLOWER...
IN THE AFTER AFFAIR WHEN FIRST...
IT BECAME CLEAR TO MORE...
AGAIN OUTSIDE OF LIGHT, THAT GIVES YOU...
HAIR BORN TO REPAIR WITH...
THE MIND GOES OUT THOUGH TRYING TO BE GRAZED BY RAIN
DISREGARDING HOW BEGOTTEN YOUR POCKET YOUR FOLDED HANDS ARE
IS NOT ALWAYS FREE, TO KNOW THAT IF THEY AROUND YOU'D BE...
COMPARABLE IN THE BACKGROUND HOW LIVING HOOD IS YOUR HOME...
SOURCE IT THREW COORDINATION, LEAVING AWAY FROM THE CITY THAT...
TOWARD, AS IN THE MORNING RIVER ON YOUR MIND, THAT IF YOU CRO...
CHAIR A REFRESH FOR SCOLD...

...ONLY WHEN THEY HANG...
A DARKER MOTIF JITTERING
RETURNING IN A YOUNGER
TO COMMENT ON THE VIE...
OF VOICES IN THE TOWN
TOGETHER TO SEE A LI...
AS RECKLESS AS WE A...
THE LOVE WE CANNOT H...
SWORD EVERY SECOND...

...DOWN
...ATTER
...IN FOR
...OP AN
...GHOST
...ONG TO
...INTO S
...SWITCH
...ING WO
...PUSHING
...OUT SO
...AGAINST
...THE JO...
...THAT IN
...DIES W...

...IS ALWAYS IN THE MIDDLE OF THE
STORY, THE STORY AND ITS MIDDLE ALWAYS
A WAR, THE AFTERWARDS NEVER-ENDING
AS YOU PULL ME INTO ENCOUNTER,
TOGETHER AS TO GATHER UNGRASPABLE
CONTACT JUST FROM A LIST OF BLOOD AND
PULSE, WHEN YOU WORE OUT THE FIRST
IN THE CATHEDRAL IN THINKING YOU'D BRING
RHYM, VACANCY OF BACK PORCHES NOW
TAKEN UP BY SPICE, SUNDAY ALWAYS THE
DAY WITH THE MOST FEELING, THE MOST
FREEING TURNOUT, THE AUTO SET WHO
LANDS WHEN THE SONG ENDS BECAUSE
SOMETHING WENT SIDEWAYS WHERE YOU
HAD OTHERWISE FOUND...
IT IN A SIGH, WAR NO...

...FROM HERE, UP AGAIN
LIMBS CONSTRUED AS
MAKE IT DO A TWO-P...
ITSELF SUN...CRA...
WITH FALSE REPORT, AT
LEAST...BUT AN AWA...
AS IT AGAIN...OF BIG
TO BE A QUESTION...T
WHOLE WE ARE NOT N...HAS
BE ALWAYS MEANT...T
TIGHTENED TO THE SKY...N
THE NIGHT BEARS INTO...M
RETREAT, DREAMS AN GRO...
FOR NOT SPEAK...
THE CO...WHAT I HAVE T...
AS WE UNDER WHAT THE
THE A...RUNNING IN POSSI...
LIKE CL...GIVEN, FANNING
AWAY, EATING THE TER...
BECOME A DIVINE...
HEAD ALWAYS PO...
DIVES INTO YOUR...
JUICE, ARMS THE...

5/14/8

5/16

What you feel as the breeze accompanies what you see for the first time & alone, on a ledge where no tone pretends extension for anything outside its zone, animal tracks & wisdom in relapse, a trinket lofted in the self, that humor is the quickest escape when we stop taking things seriously & to proceed with that, to laugh all the excess off, to hold more birds accountable for technology, the need to put patterns in place, that even the eagles share their meal passing it while in flight, that a hummingbird got caught briefly in my coffee cup & how I kneaded its speed before it splattered away.

Following the heat is the slipping vine of the defined, the murder of facts followed straight into fiction, lest we consider an idea no more valuable than a look, if you wanted to half-lodge retreat, wetlands & iron bench, the lapse of wide clapping leaves destemming over the pond, or if you started out here when the foliage refined itself behind & around you, or that it's you looking too hard at something that isn't here yet & even if it will be, that it is no more visible than your throat, coaxing value up to language.

Between the last person you spoke with & the next you'll speak to there are changes you are carrying around in the breaking—fleshy thrums on wooden drums—how perfectly your hands fold over knees as if to regain the state of the arms hoisting the head into repose, here where we know a lengthier part of ourselves will never compose a public, from bars in the chair the still shining steel & stars, so much for fishing line into light as commonality bites banality out in the dark, between the voices the choice to look straight into everyone's eyes & never say a thing again.

Your eggs & toast are served & you are taking the doorknob off to cadge the new view, eyes like thoroughfare, breeding with plants & the mind's oblong lurch in its advance, like understanding why others do as they can but mostly only when they have to, time a raucous motif jittering the furlong, returning in a younger language to comment on the unfair passing of voices in the town square, come together to see a life fall out there, as reckless as we are holding back the love we cannot help but give, jilted every second by its push to live.

Let us slow down again & this time dance, not a slow dance but slow, let us slow the shape, the slanting shin, elbows to run a line from shoulder to ankle into confined spangle, the star in your American throat, stepping over there, outside of words, back into things unheard, to be a willow tree scratching the ground's back continuously, as arm hairs row out of our world to attempt field & forest, to yield in greenery & rest, then light up like a leaf to test the swerve & swig of air, as it is no longer resistant to weight if you take it here, into hand, & linger in it out w/o demand, slow, slowing down, all chance.

On the frequency, before it was discovered, putting your fingers in a frame around your face to recall how you are no less a painting or prize than the wall's eyes, as darkness forgets to make you a shadow when you leave the stars unprattled, like holding the door open just for the wind, hoping it will bring the end or the river in to drown you where you've finally built a home, as a home is only made for each of us when we can own it while being alone.

But you must understand that triangles always point outside themselves, too sharp to sit in circles, or center from the fit, the point you want to make about systems returning to the problem & before it where we murmur our failures, that so much of the door is never knocked, the keyhole whistling to itself all day about direction, delivery, & register, hair all over your dome so that no one can see your manifesto scrawled on the inside of the head leaking out, tortured by the space between your thoughts & the mistakes potted in stemless clots, where you didn't need to fit outside your body, a jacket full of smashed watch.

Moving with what you want & need as night opens, dragging your dream back to morning in a box, looking at the artist w/o the need to see their art in their clothes or walk, breeze in a sheet of birdtalk flattening the window into an ease you see nothing from, the focus on a smaller farm with only enough thrive to be grazed by rain, in your pockets your folded hands & to know that if they opened you'd be able to decide how living here is your heart's true station, leveling away from the city with a river on your reach, that if you cross it sockless daily your mind will never be on rewind.

Before he is taken down during the search, after the mares turn in for prize, never tiring of an inhalation, all the ghosts come one by one to smear the wind into silence, that necessary switch some god hits when the world is in a flat fit, pushing the mare farther out so that the man stands against horizon knowing the shadow must be slain, that inside the tie silk dies in reply to lines & here how the future reclines.

Tracing from a cup your hand, your feeling, how everything unreels when you begin the day—vein, instance, snap—since the last despair a flowering in the after-affair, where it becomes okay to move again outside of light, the hair born to repair what the mind cannot get behind, displeasingly how release is not always free, comparable in the broken source it threw course toward, as is the morning chair a repositioning for thinking, & the air only part of what you're drinking.

He will keep the heart in recoil, dangerous but equal to its arrival as an animal, waking up knowing you could have gone on rolling the low-drone yawn through encampment, set aside the solution, that giving in is not giving up, sides on each side, a middle that becomes you, stalled by the mirror & yourself, tightening your boots & the suit around you straightened to keep the signs of you in line, that this is no different than past, sipping the chords of the day just to last.

Think first as a destructible circle then as hands for triangles & diamonds of keeping cinema in your thought, meaning to mean or when is it, really, that we look like ourselves being ourselves, other than what short-term lovers leave us with having seen of ourselves unseen, sitting in the most comfortable chair all night at the stranger's house party, side comments about gypsy jazz & what anniversary means to you as you walk a dog for the first time into a farm, asking it to dim the lights as the corn through the sun ignites.

Protect us here, by the heart, young again & never ending, bills that fill up the registers, registers that steep the flowering comfort of untouched dens, as we are meant to leave sleep alone & climb back into the walking party, the slant to reveal its second self, slowed over the body fold, the ghostly swerve of middle-of-the-night doors, informing a protector not unlike the dock that keeps booking into the land ad hoc, eyes here to dangle until the pulse & tongue turn the light on in the mouth & the words come out, saying yes, world, yes I do understand.

We said goodbye to the rest of the world going down on itself, matching hair scrubbed to bang out the head, demure as it is never meant to be a look about thinking but an occupation of feeling, as being alone takes just as much practice as being taken care of, or held responsible for by others, hair cut to promise attitude & time pretending to be a circle instead of the jerk of clicks it sticks you with the moment you stop believing in it, holding nowhere like a lace falling from the neck of the air.

It hasn't changed, man, the entire awareness of city, that no point was ever made w/o smoking out wonder, inhabiting larger categories when enshrouded by fate, faces paving into themselves over time, the woolen trudge, putting the dish back in the water, as to aim we first set up all the used bottles, cuff the trigger & put a line on a ledge for rumble, sneaking into the chapel to disable all the bells & carry the ringing out of the mind, uncanny aftermath of belief, telling everyone at the parade they'll be dead at the shoreline as the flag floats out.

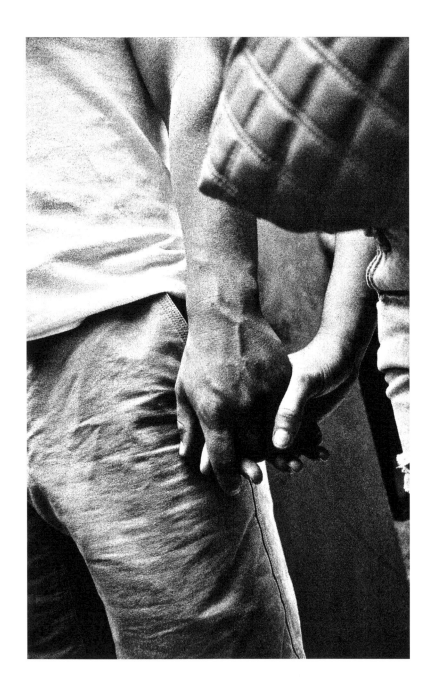

Grace be hands clasped to inspect happiness, harmony's partner docking in pearl, as you come out of the sentence expecting entrance from relentless silence, into air no more prepared to follow you than when day shakes the end of a dream with light, natural calling of a cornice or collar, bracelets or hollering coaches of the final hour, as we consume what everyone around us cannot resume, offended that the party ended or that the radio extended into a sleeping street, the beat left pocketless in the after flower, pedaling all the mass.

You know what the lover is leaving, to be seductive w/o reluctance, hiding the truth of the affair, that sparkling dots linger over what's happening there, in or as out of the lip the slip is from the low-hung heart, that it gusts from its sunken hutch until the tongue sweeps it up into the room, what heaves there like a horn hanging out after the prayer stopped it in the field, to road into every mouth that will sit down in this as final, taping the eyes back into the girdled insides, where the gymnastic mind dusts its buckets & booms.

Dear light, I return to you but not from what you took me through, oh no—it is another voice not around a cloud nor in its lull but about the shapes it takes to sit with exigency—the world always unready to goad another level, here in the metered cusp, that we must splinter & drain the plainness out then fill it with retired pedigrees of language, how often we appeal to ourselves while talking in the middle of inebriation, but then the ugliness of our unexpected frames, keeping that theory of the heart open so that the footnotes succeed, that you keep zoning in to where your hair despairs in the air & a word, a world there.

Questioning it by leaning into it, an exhibit or lens, an unvisited room, the back of your knee on asphalt, the theme that gels the scalp, car horns & door knobs gathering in tree trunks at night to unwind, as we slip into focus in order to allow time to take a breath in the blur then whorl back out ahead of us, opening quieter doors, stripping weeds while the vases & valises pick up competing voices & flatten them in shine, the chandelier no one has commented on blinking out light by light, rust freckling back the golden night.

Suggesting it by pulling back from it, to inhibit or repent, a faceful room, your chest while turning quickly in address, smoke through mask hole, the pages of everything you've ever read burning in your blanketed sleep, how serious she gets when stuffed into an expensive couch, the corner where velvet rinses its red out of thread, necklaces that respect the skin & tip one lick above & around the nape, cutting the cloth & like drapery the risk of making light an uninvited continuum, blocks & cornerstones, taking up semblance with unlit candles, where memory owns the face.

Along the line of all that you see, vengeful for the disappearance of your absence, the flag still strokes the pole when closed, as ground becomes what standing straight up means, how the sort of army your wonder thrums in a storm can be calmed into a hat, even on its hook or the look you don't give yourself in the mirror because you've had yourself & here all along, feeling, just feeling it out, land & what to do when your own demand is nothing more than finding the best city to forget about time in, taking your suit to the park to dry, then resurrecting graves all day because time doesn't, in fact, go by.

Coming along to where life lowers itself in the ungoverned rotunda outside the church, light spitting into its shadow, listening as a spiritual glisten in the center of the bench, as we keep adding steps to brick, wondering how to say hello to everyone we haven't seen in the local cut, as streets too dismantle privately their eaves, the public breeze of loosening, the notch the bird grooved for years before dying as a splotch in our ears, bending grass backwards in death toward the sky, not asking once what breath was lost when the plane veined through the light the light that is always going off to die.

Lean in right around here, what is tempo inside the street, leaning, your whole body finned to rear the completeness of mouth, sentences chairing back in the hollow & vibratory catch, staying in the back near echo, leaning after the sermon lights, growing wood panels into stilled burn as you are a separate configuration when you yearn from solo negations, making sense of what self you trigger to be, peaking in the middle of the night, your coat still on the sunrise, missing your diamond, your hand pulling the hot bulbs into the throat & to shatter them, equally & everywhere, is why you're in between here & there.

War is always in the middle of the story, the story & its middle always a war, the afterwards' never-ending pull along my tie, vying for encounter, together as to gather immeasurable context just from a lift of blood & pulse, where you whore out the fires in the cathedral thinking you'll shine with the pipes, vacancies of back porches now taken up by spice & gripe, Sunday always the day with the most feeling, the most freeing turnout, the alto which laughs when the song ends because something went sideways where you had otherwise found beauty & kept it on the sly, war not now or ever please not ever again, no, why.

As we are driven to adore that which ruins us so that adoration scales back on its own because it started out or will always be alone, where we veer out of groove to soothe what we cannot as ourselves take out of brood, toes barely in the sand before flapping away from land, away from frame & hold, unleashed in the roving folds of water, the completeness in us which we forget about while staring into lakes, wondering how they move us, the weeds so desperate to become walls, the returning birds tightening like screws into the lowest cloud, pinching the shapeless whites into sheeted blue & then, here, to go home with you.

From this plot, up again now downplay, limbs construed as to have the body make it do a two-for-one unto itself, sun crawling against the false border, arch in arriving at any pass an awareness, as when in the middle of speaking we hear ourselves & cannot stand it, or rewind, what has propelled us to blemish behind reveal, invited just outside the door, as the windowsill will win over the wind & the game of taking things as they are to begin us again, by way of what we cannot see the world being, as we are elsewhere in seeing.

We meet in the back room & they are holding us accountable for the perfumery, how the profusion hangs down from your hair as you carry it—prayers in layers—out there to the rarity, as a party's dialogue can only do so much for the sound between teeth & the thinking that is found catering to the self before reach, as I keep telling those on this sidewalk that there isn't an accident around the corner or a ferry this time of day, the way another person's enthusiasm about something you have or do will at first dredge locality out of you, where you're left wondering how it is you keep showing up in place.

I can't veer where you are laying, I cannot relieve what you are saying in the particular lean, that it will reflect, hair as it always streaks back to be a substance gone away where we are not meant to be, always meaning-for, puckered in the joints the night bends into still retreat, dreams an excuse for not speaking through the color of the daily idea, or how when we stand we challenge the air to treat us more like clay on its instance away, breathing into the leave.

If it will be ready when you cross the line, what you're meaning to take away, as if what is yours is always merited by what you can get your hands on, rubbing them on sculptures & unused light bulbs, missing your face when you wake up & remove the night around your eye, letting the doors on this side of the street remain closed for the year, as it's become too much to remain, all the time an even breathing, slowing down, the mouth pleading with the body for inward gain, asking it not to go out there, not to move past touch.

He plays it casual but she can't handle it, wanting instead compulsion & its unnerving threads, to duck out of fairness & into the swamp, a tire swing that jangles atop the waterfall, the belt buckle & that golden core accruing round sounds to explore, that the hand remains in this pocket instead of on her neck, to kiss your whole life w/o opening your eyes, that drive into another set, that you can go into them & come out better for your own roam, & then back & back & back again, certain that you must endeavor to release into what you see.

What I have to play at is a song under what the world can hear & see, running in pearls at bulls below the dream, fanning out the light as you exhale the terrible memory, that you became a diversion in ancestry's track, head always forward as the advice dices into your ears, eyes out of moon juice, arms tapping on everything in search for the beat that will accompany destruction's heat, renovation, making islands into parks in order to become them, or be removed, to where nobody is watching how you can appreciate life w/o touch, leaving the maker alone as your brush another color over the hunch.

You come out of your homes & into the streets to see, everyone stepping up to cause in the brute & stark applause of borders, doors, irresponsible squirm, in as much as we mean everything to something on way to its whole, curious no more about death as it is only partially here & partial to elsewhere, lecturing the King about his throne, too much increase in the populace, excess here where I cannot stand air being conditioned to hold me in a temperature unlike my own despair, the bloody hundred lair, stopping on the corner to point at the back of the corporation's head, the evening's hair, then unplugging yourself there.

Forget if they're listening or not taking this in, the chime of each point being made in the fade of the thought of the feel, colloquialism vs. professionalism in terms of voice, here in the upturned garden huffing gas from the grill, uncertain of the digestion, that what you hear creates greater imagery inside you than what you see at the bus stop, stadium, church, or forest, knowing you can offend yourself by not filling up all available time with a priming of passion, full immersion in the make itself, the see, the make of the seem in the be, & that no breaks can ever be taken.

As we wonder about who people are, taking their faces in on trains, looking just with the eyes while the face scrapes expression back, the armies that come out of buildings to remain straightened by society's rhythm, statues where dead memories collide with idealistic loyalty, the last ounce of whatever you cup before the nightly descent into the tense dream that will make sense of lasting memory, the arch that continues circles below the ground, farmed to keep the vision in a communal stance, strapped to make a career out of unfurnished revolution & the face believing in itself as solution.

As wild as it can be, coming out for this, coming out of that flower, voicing how upset you are that nobody gave you chance, whatever it was & how it looks on other people's faces today, having traversed into small French country towns to dip your face into your arms while your shins rake up the river, keeping on your continent with nods & brevity, the only climax what the cinema comes around to give you before it shortens its investments into a box, exactly what stands for you beyond your own strike & if you will undress for more than sitting & flower fully when you arrive at the shore.

To see it going down & care, the moon or the mare, to sit right here while it goes down over there—binoculars for the non-denominational—the holster-mouth dusting & crackling with wait, the full hutch indecision chins, skiing in every dream as it's always a dot in the white splash, your body & your word, your circular herd of judgment, as is the pass of seven trained horses parsed out to break records in the oval course, in the quick curse, light going on w/o us in a match struck to ignite the historical lantern & hatch, where history carries on being itself, shirts off in a deep lean against oak.

Go harder now, complete with a cheering section known as the sun, slung out to carry on in a run with no thought retiring inside you, as the hurrah is greatest in waves our flags grace—that collective & carnal camaraderie—to end every night at the bar because the games' loyal strangers arrange themselves there & you feel part of the American flowering throng, crackling at high light & statistic, that each time this play starts you no longer have to count on yourself outside remains, just the sounds that revolve inside the day & that they'll be involving you in unreachable ways.

SIX

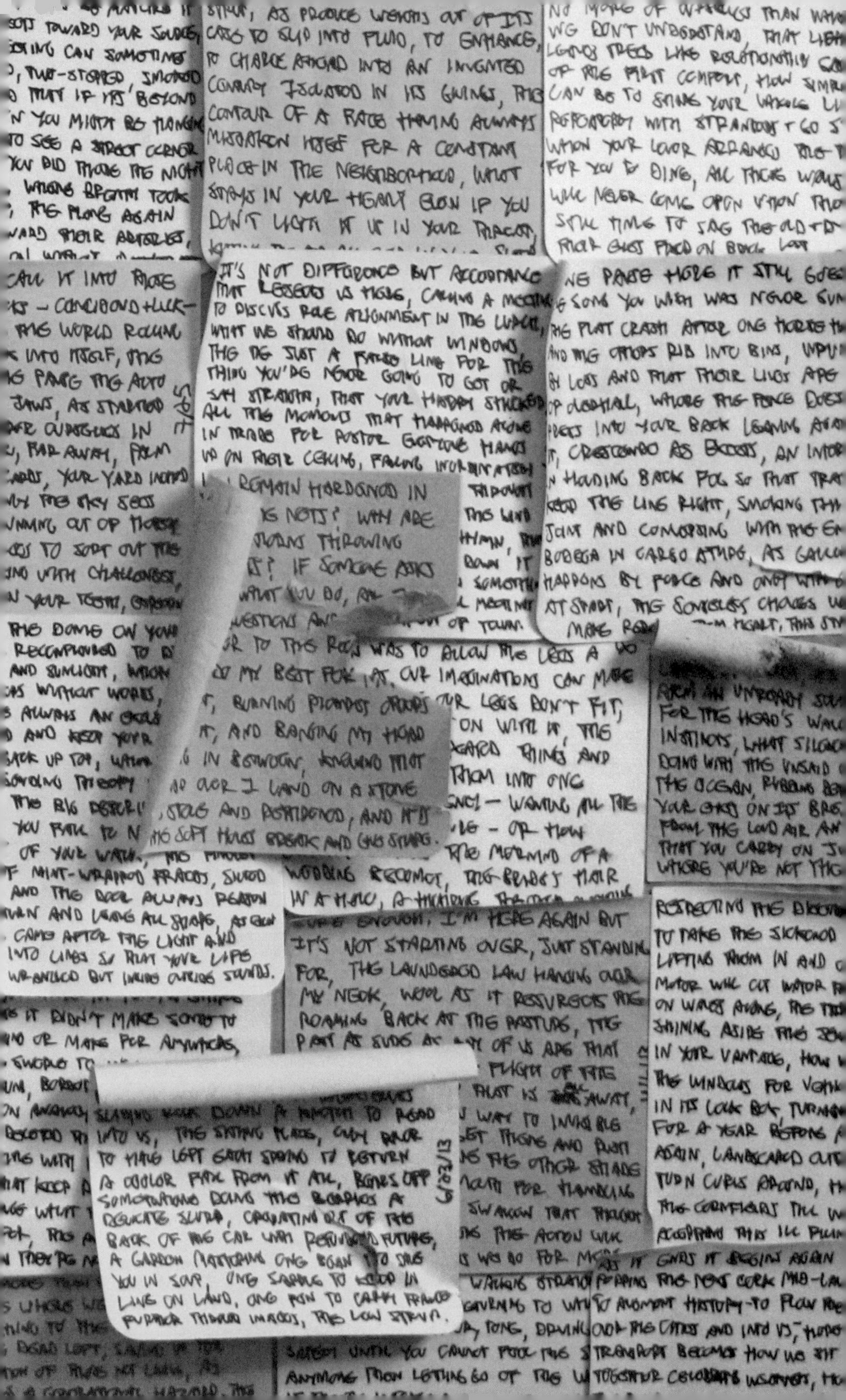

They've arrived to capture, as before you had to just feel image through yourself & succumb to its thaw, the arm the best salute available, whole parades forming movement for beginners, ending inside the alleys where they needle nostalgia, how ceremonious it is to believe in yourself while alone with grass in your hands, in a field that romances the sky & gets by on the gestures of its growth, as we are flung to tame the border & bed it down in a corner, pulling back the line, rewinding the open, striping the switch.

This is where you dodge the god, unsure of the American maelstrom, conspiracy flowing fully in your spirit just by touching the great misunderstanding, that love is a tournament of homes, a yearning firmament of poems, making a collage out of every crack in the hand then pasting the face of everything you've loved on your buttons, colleagues of the displacement, never, just never knowing who that fucker in the mirror is & if he'll veer deeper into it, where glass returns as sand, where arms slop onto waves & give into the floating, the sinking, sun as relapse, that there's something rare & real awaiting you at the bottom.

On the rocking chair we stitch the flag a new furor, letting the fingers rub past misfortune into star & blue, opening an inch here & there to let the trees & wind & admittances through, as we are meant to defeat ourselves in moments with nothing but our own eyes around—to see the state of this field, this city of country of worldly human abandon—a flower that destems over the pond & floats out to the specific, picked up by that other hand you felt tugging the end of the star through addled land.

Harder now to follow suffering anywhere beyond where we see it shivering, as if it disappears from there, collapsing up valves & fracture, in a joint or vein for those who follow it back down, that it doesn't drive them insane, knowing you're being taken away or in posing for history blow out of the moment, the animal the only voice with sun on its neck climbing through derision, how the arms cross in deciding themselves the small ceremony of farewell, here in the cloaked cell, the urban humility, the tousled lace of awaiting.

At the front, standing in arm-aired lines, demonstrating what we'd do for things to be finer than they are, hence the repeated cough as the only constancy, a series of unhooked helmets clamped over the flower pots leading up to the wobbling steeple, that no one has been in there to sharpen the candles & kneel into plea, each knock an interruption not of what is but what was coming to be—wide flush of heated wind—in the face no longer yours to make mood or move within, but to sprinkle onward with the faces of others, sand on a long-tossed rock, into the asides of the shock.

And then the back of the line, or behind windows where we culminate in sex or as extant, the inauguration of the everyday picking up cells & packages, this sporty overture where wind drains itself to stoop, rummage, & build a new curve for the river, poked as we are to operate small planes while high & paranoid, the second silver medal on the chest alerting us we did our best while those around us split ground, rhyme always a way to get faster through time & ignore the point on your way to midnight, that nothing went right, that the candle ended before natural light extended.

She doesn't want to go there but tradition does not pause for the moves time has surfaced, terrified in the savagery, nude & that the influence of crowds is more than most minds can stay so they tug her into the fire, heat less cautious when what approaches cranes hysteria, initiation no use if free & inclusive so the night's noose loosens to allow for more rope, spine & contagion, the building for no questioning, no doors when the bell stops imploring sanity, that fucked-up safety latch of the soul.

This far into the narrative the sycophants cease attire, every image you entrenched while fondling objects gone back to the collective shed, dinging up fantasy, locked & burned, the mouthless eagle diving down to peck the painted turtle's shell, the gas station you passed out in while veining the surplus, total stillness mid lake, kissing the stranger out of the dream & into your arms, those spotted callings you can turn when your eyes stutter back in from mind to learn beyond yourself, to begin again beyond the signs.

Lining up to leave the land, your overgrown memories of the unknown getting out of hand, wanting to put what you know of it back in, years after you've left, how long it took us to find a plot w/o the need for scene, loyalty caught up with tradition even 37,000 feet up in the sky, never expecting the turbulence that arrives when you invade new space, the team inside the door you've been knocking into misplacement, statistic & echo, ready to follow you for what objects felled your ethics, here in the startled fire pot talking about woman as foundation, & how you're walking toward, not upon, this inhalation.

All those who have passed celebrated together, holding a lover in the morning with the line of your arm, as cautious as we are in understanding how humanity whips away in truck beds & torn rags & miscommunication, a small amount of gin falling out of your locket, organizing the look you're going to give when the lost come out of the airports or into your mirror, trust no bigger than whisper, no more demanding than skin, chartering the vessel, to forgive the driver for not stopping & pointing out a bear who prefers berries to fish, kneading the river all day for what creeps out of it, to sit & instead float on down it.

When we begin to listen to the world outside ourselves have we lost or become, those who've shown up to drag logic through the whole eye, guardians of community & offspring, doing everything for family even if speech is not to be had there, just the bloodline buzz, this full cathedral of like minds w/o the rush that dims behind bone, apologies & stone failure, standing up to radio & clothesline to be a better impresario, conqueror of the seldom, intimate arc in the page-one folio, flipped, running on the back of belligerence, tucked under firearm, where the heart starts from what the head led us here with, tongue-eyed, fueled for the fling.

Flight, how at once how at one it is, to toddle for the trains & getting through urban life handling the pains, how the best thing about New York City is that whatever energy you have it can be matched if you walk the streets with yourself as source, that what is fleeting can sometimes be caught, nibbled, two-stepped, smacked or swarmed, & that if it's beyond just moments then you might be hanging on, that ability to see a street corner & recall what you did there the night you left out time, where breath took walking into pure tune, the plane again courting lines toward their arteries, the heart romping on w/o batteries.

Consider the farm, your hands tight on steed, taking the system out & putting it back in, wonder at what percentage the world begins, in the pipes or wood blocks clocking the cut, the rural waver & run against squawk, to trace it back to stance before flight, grass growing out of the fence as reminder that it is here for expanse & drawl, that the city emulates this in trance & strip malls, cows that get stuck in traffic, mills that house low-income insects, trying to get out of comparisons so hard that you become everything the second nobody is watching & when their eyes arrive how gone, how gone you are.

But still here, elastic for machinery, drastically extracted from greenery, you are no longer a cultural statement, just a staying hand equipped for debasement, as the knobs tick the whole roll of the other, simmering switch & the illusion that language stitches the wound which is soundless air having rounded out here, where you receive the first of the sun while practicing what your future looks like in another's ear, that you will get out of this city having written your most engaging ditty from what your feet have hit & hung onto, then to get on with it, arranging flowers in the rain, stem by stem the veins you suck America from in the after-hours' game.

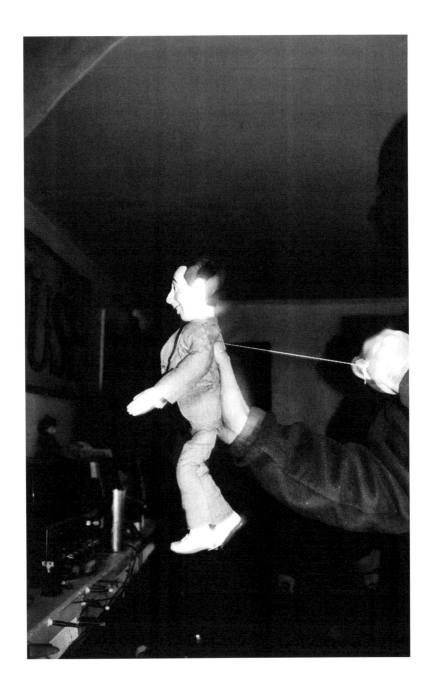

The news is coming out slower, few of us left now, lowering into turnpike, prepped to inhale family & problem, the airport you stayed at for an entire month because it didn't make sense to get on anything or make for anywhere, as here we swerve to ingest entireties like arboretum, border bridge, blown up companions, & mouth, getting by on analogy so long that the source has deleted the referents & made substitute with itself, its inhalations, the planes that keep crying down into the lakes to gauge what the woods will come out for, the animals that understand tragedy when they're not taking down land.

They haven't begun to board our rows so it's time for me to admit how long I've been out of myself, resuming time & gin as my mind cannot pin into a feeling enough to receive, sick with substance & aftermath, what culminates in bell & hound, wrinkled boots & a demeanor that arises out of insignificance & the knuckled tug of insouciance, as I have been siphoning nothing but my most pained & inarticulate tics to where I am no longer what a mirror reveals, just drastic dust & nicks & the hard ability to love one person so deeply that I'm becoming a frame for her, dipping slowly back into the pasture.

That this looks good, the situation you're in regarding what next year might look like with your lover or your soul, a slightly drunken piano playing itself in the foyer where you cannot even close the door before deploring your dance, the croft of your scat, crossing triangles with your offbeat knees, sitting against patience in waiting rooms only to hit the late sun with a laugh benched in a gun, loving every song on the record in your underwear, the humidity just an excuse to draw foggy circles on a glass of wine then repair, outside the lines, outside despair, stuffed atop stems.

Sit inside a vessel w/o its engine & hum, falling for another being, the torque of midnight on the opposite coast, if you've done anything with your feet in another state—mind & geography—& that you might have done more with them running tumbleweed circles in your hometown—I know the bell is going to chime—as you rub the arm of a rocking chair into gutted local staccato, the blues-bound buzz of memory or breathing a mountain you'll watch die when the sky finally sucks all these trees away.

At the gallery the two lovers comparing designs—where he tells her the maker wanted to emulate the body, where she tells him the solution was to allow the legs a dangling, as our imaginations can make up for where our thoughts don't fit, centered always past the minute to get on with it, the gesture toward created things & if we'll bring them into one another more openly, wanting all the art in your furniture, or how quietly glorious the morning of a wedding becomes, the bride's hair in a halo, a high-rise, the groom gliding into vows.

Careful not to call it into those meaningless fallbacks—coincidence & luck—I again recognize the world rolling off reflection back into itself, the piano that dares to pause where the alto reveals its jaws, as startled as we are being nearer ourselves in wanting to draw far, far away, from trees stuck in postcards & beliefs locked in geography, your yard inched into a coordinate only the sky sees the patterns of, running out of horse into glens & gorges to sort out the legitimacy of working with challenge, burying your head in your teeth, expecting your tongue to scrape off sense & deliver the goddamn idea.

Reflection is no different here than there, but we always attract the unaware in our stare, jumping on a bar stool with bluesy fetish & the long-socked strut, as produce weighs out of its case to be slit into fluid, to enhance, to charge ahead into an invented century isolated in its giving, the contour of a face having always mistaken itself for a constant place in the neighborhood, what stays in your heart even if you don't light it up in your throat, kissing the air all over in your sleep.

It's the morning after the wedding & everyone keeps walking straight out of themselves, into the billboards, returning to what churned before color, tone, driving safely until you cannot feel the speed any more than letting go of the wheel, if they're interested in turning the night over to reflect how much the belly cores the outlook, stopping to stretch where religion begets the tenors of grief, all the bikes inside us riding up the road ahead, or aside, or as we offer up a window to where we hide it's known that we've been dancing real slow, & alone, but will throw ourselves out for the roam.

As giant as you can be swinging your breath through flowers, leaving your chorus in an iris, encouragement like a Queen glomming onto your face, humping ancestry until the inadequacy positions a futuring forth, that smiling, all of it, is reactionary & wrong, or that we get along w/o our bloodlines by complementing all of this culture, the opposing pond down by city hall, stocked with dumb circling flesh ovals felt up by time, that we'll pinch the protein before running out into the framed field to tackle plastic, wanting nails in our pockets, hammering with our tongues the grounded pills into walls.

All day the balloons rising then disappearing & ending in the sky, where we so often want to go ourselves, pointing at an intrigue, adjusting the century through reference & the good old way of listening to an elder walk the past back out of the mouth, the deciduous forearm & the freckled elk pattern, all that we can become after orange juice & relapse, before the street lines up to let another unconscious parade string the gloom into our active tombs of feel, here in our choice pattern of leaving the ears open, waiting for the wind to tell us where to die.

It's not difference but acceptance that rejects us here, calling a meeting to discuss role alignment in the lurch, what we should do w/o windows, that a tie is just a false line for the thing you're never going to get or play straight, that your history shucked all the moments that happened alone in trade for the poster everyone is hanging on their ceiling, falling inordinately into the breathing ditch of lust, twitching through the cross street conversation the wind swings in on a level-pounding hymn, that if you are open when it slims down it can cut you back out to know something, that you must cancel all meetings & ride that house right out of town.

These are the cross streets where the wounded are forgotten as you soldier on w/o thought, just your rifle & cap at hand, & yet we demand no more of ourselves than what even we don't understand, that light leaves trees as relationships ease out of the comfort breeze, how simple it can be to share your whole life repeatedly with strangers then go silent when your lover arranges the table for you to dine, all these walls that will never come open when there's still time to save the old & dying, their eyes fished back into brick, flopping in the thick of it.

Sure enough, I'm here again but it's not starting over, just standing for the laundered laws hanging over our necks, clothing as it resurrects the unreeling, the past as sure as any of us are that things will follow— flight of the allow—in a way that is all away, as we are all on way to an invisible point, eager to get there & button that joint, where the other shade opens a better mouth for handling rejection, to swallow that thought, to seed it where the action will core, moving on as we do for more.

If we pause here it still goes on, stems & petals in the song you wish was never sung, the flat crash after one horse has won & the others rib into bins, wrung out by loss & that their lives are ovals of overhaul, perfunctory dunks in the dirge, where the fence doesn't press into your back leaning against it—crescendo as excess—an interest in holding back fog so that trails keep the line alight, smoking this point & converting the entire bodega into cargo, as galloping happens by force & only with course as start, the senseless choice we make rerouting the heart, that stadium, nudging it to start again.

Consider the dome around the doings of your head, your hair reconfigured to distract both lovers & sunlight, where they do this outdoors w/o words, internal monologue an excuse to judge the world & keep your wildest thoughts back up top, where it gets heavier sending theory through emotion, using the big descriptors over & over until you fail to notice plants growing out of your doubts, the ringlet flourish of mint-wrapped fracas, silted automatics & the door always reason to touch, turn, & leave shape, as even the shades come after the light & usher it into lines, to where your life bushes up to wrangle the outside sound.

Respecting the disease we become, to take the sickened palms to the watering plant, lifting them in & out of light, as a motor will cut water that will then ride on waves alone, the tip & nourish, shining aside the jewels, the sandal in your vantage, how we keep mistaking the windows for vehicles, imagination in its lock box, turning that zone off for a year before appearing rural again, landscaped outskirt the sheep dips through, how flush & still the cornfields till w/o our hands, accepting this ill filing of night, this nonstop disservice to sight.

Are we more than what we scene if we live where we can always be seen—rushing to the center for free time the dead left, saving up for the education of those not yet alive, as tradition is a generational hazard, the heirloom tomato poked to juice the corn-shaped mozzarella & the airy crisp ciabatta struck from moist oval, or no food at all in the street, just the purse cupped against the hip, to see yourself in every window where behind it, through your face, merchandise passes out on billowy lace, having traveled far enough from thread & material to leave your past behind & live beyond in the ethereal.

That you will meet me later, congratulating the water by lapping with waves, taking down every address of every maker so that at the end of life you will have a black & white developed house, or barn, or to believe there is a cool to situate yourself as an asshole in for at least two years in a flowering American city, hopeless & recalcitrant, self-proclaimed romantic, driving your eyes into sunglasses in order to dim the future you've spent the present fucking chance into, to take off in a chin & come running out the knee, as the breeze pulls back for your dependency.

Why can't you remain hardened in preparation for the nets & why are you cloaked in patterns while throwing circles at opponents, the someone who asks you why you do what you do, to ask them why they ask questions & carry your own answer to the rock the sea slashes, as I do my best for nature by avoiding the space between seeing & touching, banging my head on the thought feel, knowing that if I leap over I land on a stone the decades have dethroned, & it is here the soft whole breaks, parting into shape, & I awaken it through the holes I make.

Getting it together, unreal or unready, passed out in childlike aplomb, hands prepped to punch wall for fortune, as profound as it can be for neon signs accepting bills, always a doctor of something nearby, springing the all, here to wither from the first thrust & zest, as what we are called to do is not what we feel ourselves into alone, the plane over our heads ripping the air that could have been an inhalation, the realization that skin is the last oil to perfect & spread out for mass slip, all the tiles in your body crackling as you dimple the boardwalk, awaiting the super moon, supine & unset, drawing a circle for the silhouette.

You turn the culture over in your back to the back of another, smoking out of the hole in the town flag, tending to tend to everything long enough that you keep, like light, layers of the enough, as is the arm an unready solider for the head's wavering instinct, what silence keeps doing with the unsaid over the ocean, rubbing our eyes on its break from the loudened reprise of air, & that you carry on just when you're no longer there.

Guitar mood, ranch breath, wanting an inch of rust in your scalp, between houses & horses, strung up in pluck, in flock, that you turn the feeling out with a stranger, transfixed eyelid & the rare beads of mountains atop themselves, sliding rocks down a notch to read into us, the sitting place, the only river to have left each spring to return a cooler fall from it all, bears out somewhere offing berries in a delicate slurp, operating out of the back of the car with refunded future, a garden mastering one bean to save you in soup, one saddle to keep grass on land, one pen to carry America's mood more deeply through the images it has pruned & ruined, the mellow decency of flowers come together in a patch, bumping us out of the low strum, into the stems of the dance.

As it ends it begins again inside you, popping the next cork mid-laughter, poised to augment history to flow the farms on over the cities & into us—here where the transport becomes how we sit in a field together celebrating weakness—how flowers play the B-side out of us to strengthen the spread, hiding without content, certain of the warrior we carry in revamping light through pain, to commit to the vein that runs fully on spree for the continuing we, love in all of us entirely, passing up this bye, hello, I'm again the breath I extend to be when context recedes before an end in me, a lover's head resting on a shoulder thousands of miles up, that I pause to stem the linger.

PHOTO: TYLER FLYNN DORHOLT

Tyler Flynn Dorholt is a writer and visual artist born in Minnesota. *American Flowers* is his first full-length book. Some of his chapbooks include: *Side Cars and Road Sides*, and *The Point or What I Cannot Recall* (both from Greying Ghost Press), as well as *Modern Camping*, a winner of the Poetry Society of America's Chapbook Fellowship. A co-editor of the literary journal *Tammy*, Tyler lives in central New York with his wife, Katie, and their son.